Chinese Lyricists
of the Seventeenth Century

Chinese Lyricists
of the Seventeenth Century

DAVID R. MCCRAW

University of Hawaii Press

Honolulu

© 1990 University of Hawaii Press
All Rights Reserved
Printed in the United States of America
90 91 92 93 94 95 5 4 3 2 1

Library of Congress Cataloging-in-Publication Data
Mc Craw, David R., 1954–
Chinese lyricists of the seventeenth century /
David R. Mc Craw.
p. cm.
Includes bibliographical references.
ISBN 0-8248-1279-4 (alk. paper)
1. Chinese poetry—Ch'ing dynasty, 1644–1912—
History and criticism. I. Title.
P12327.M4   1990
895.1'14809—dc20   90-10899
CIP

University of Hawaii Press books are printed
on acid-free paper and meet the guidelines
for permanence and durability of the Council
on Library Resources

Contents

Preface

This book is a critical study of the seventeenth-century Chinese poets who revived a dormant genre of Chinese verse and restored it to vigorous health. The book interprets, evaluates, and introduces to Western readers a valuable but sadly neglected corpus of Chinese poetry.

This work pays homage to my late mentor, Professor James J. Y. Liu, and is in fact closely modeled on his *Major Lyricists of the Northern Sung*. I have not called my own effort *Major Lyricists of the Early Qing* for two reasons. First, two of the poets I examine would have turned over in their graves; Chen Zilong died resisting the Qing, and Wang Fuzhi had inscribed as his epitaph "Last loyal servant of the Ming." I have also avoided the word "major" because, although all the poets in this volume are very good, most did not contribute as much to the development of the Chinese lyric as did their Soong predecessors.

In studying the seventeenth-century lyric, my approach is very much that of Professor Liu, who conceived of Chinese poetry as a dual exploration of worlds and language, a recasting of inner and outer experience into a complex verbal artifact. Accordingly, I have selected six authors whose lyrics most exemplified or influenced the evolution of the Qing lyric. For each author, I translate a number of lyrics to indicate the range and depth of his characteristic poetic realms. Then I analyze his use of diction, imagery, syntax, allusions, and prosody to determine what is distinctive about his verbal art. I conclude each chapter by assessing what contributions the author made to early Qing lyrics.

While following Professor Liu's example, I should also point out the several ways in which I depart from it. First, I begin each chapter with a sketch of the author's life and character, for I believe that familiarity with an artist's lived experience and personality *can* shed light on his art. Readers might object that, since poets "nothing deny and nothing affirm," their poetry is irrelevant to their lives. Even a few Chinese critics, usually so quick to equate a man and his poetry, caution that lyricists cannot be held responsible for sentiments expressed in a lyric because the lyric genre is too trivial a medium in which to "express one's intent." Still, Qing lyricists often appear to speak in a personal voice, and, while I would advise extreme caution in using the lyric as a biographical source, knowledge of a lyricist's life and character enriches our understanding of that personal voice that seems to address us from the pages of his verse.

Second, since Qing lyricists wrote in the shadow of their Soong predecessors, I have included in each chapter comparisons with earlier lyricists. These parallels sharpen our grasp of each poet's style, establish his poetic models, and help us see each poet's accomplishments in perspective.

Finally, I omit word-for-word renderings, romanization, and metrical diagrams from my translations. In fact, I discuss lyrical prosody only cursorily, partly because Professor Liu has already treated it in detail, partly because it is a complex subject that does not lend itself to an interlingual context.

In selecting lyrics for translation, I have tried to include poems that exemplify each poet's range of styles. Readers who have just savored the highlights of a particular poet's oeuvre may find my critical judgments too harsh. I must beg those readers to remember that my judgments are based on comparisons between poets' complete works. Some will object that my selections are not entirely representative. I can only concur; presenting what I feel are a poet's finest works seems a lesser evil than burdening the reader with more "typical" but mediocre verses.

In translating lyrics, I have tried to steer a middle course between translations that are literal but obscure and those that are clear but unfaithful to the original's form, content, and style. Longer lines (of five syllables or more) begin close to the left margin, while shorter lines are indented farther. "Lead-in" words that govern more than one line of verse extend to the left margin; the line of verse to which they "belong" and subsequent lines are indented. Finally, I have used terminal punctuation to indicate a rhyme in the original text. This means that occasionally a period will punctuate an incomplete sentence, but it helps suggest that a "line" of lyric verse is an entity often more metrical than syntactical in nature.

It remains only to explain a few of the conventions I follow in this book. First, I have reduced footnotes to a minimum. My preference is to explain well-known allusions and bits of lore; sinologists do not need citations for these, and laymen need explanations, not citations to texts they cannot read. I reserve such citations for more obscure sources that even sinologists might find unfamiliar. Second, I use the *pinyin* system of romanization, with a few exceptions. For example, since Nalan Singde's name is so well-known in that spelling, I have decided not to change it to Xingde. I refer to the Soong dynasty (960–1279) in order to avoid confusion with the English word "song" and with another Song dynasty (420–479).

In all other particulars, my treatment hopes to emulate that of Professor Liu, to whom I owe an immense debt of gratitude. I only wish that he might have lived to guide this work, for then it would be a far better book than the one you now read. Thanks are also due Irving Lo, Richard Lynn, and Cheng Ching-mao, all of whom made invaluable comments on early draft manuscripts. I apologize for not having made better use of their wise counsels.

Abbreviations

CHCB: Tang Guizhang, ed. *Cihua Congbian*.

CJLWJ: Chen Weisong, *Chen Jialing Wenji*.

CJZJ: Chen Yuyi, *Jianzhai Shiji*.

CSJC: *Congshu Jicheng*.

CSXP: Wang Xiaoyu, *Wang Chuanshan Xuepu*.

CZYNP: Wang Yun, *Chen Zhongyu Nianpu*.

CZYQJ: Chen Zilong, *Chen Zhongyu Quanji*.

DSYD: Hung Yeh, *A Concordance to the Poetry of Du Fu*.

GZCJ: Wang Fuzhi, *Guzhuo Chuji*.

GZEJ: Wang Fuzhi, *Guzhuo Erji*.

HHL: Chen Weisong, *Huhailou Ciji*.

HYSIS: Harvard-Yenching Sinological Index Series.

LDSX: Ding Ying, *Lidai Shixuan*.

MCJC: Wu Weiye, *Meicun Jiacang Gao*.

PSTC: Zhu Yizun, *Pushuting Ci*.

PSTJ: Zhu Yizun, *Pushuting Ji*.

QSC: Tang Guizhang, *Quan Songci*.

RJCH: Wang Guowei, *Renjian Cihua (Poetic Remarks in the Human World)*.

SBBY: *Sibu Beiyao*.

SBCK: *Sibu Congkan*.

SKTY: Ji Yun, *Siku Quanshu Zongmu Tiyao*.

TSSJY: Gao Buying, *Tang Song Shi Juyao*.

WCSS: Wang Fuzhi, *Wang Chuanshan Shiwen*.

WSJL: Wu Weiye, *Wushi Jilan*.

XXYC: Wang Fuzhi, *Xiao Xiang Yuanci*.

XZC: Chen Zilong, *Xiangzhen Ci*.

YSCJ: Nalan Singde, *Yinshui Ci Jian*.

ZZYD: Hung Yeh, *A Concordance to Zhuangzi*.

O N E

Introduction

The focus of this book is poetry, not cultural history. But to understand how seventeenth-century Chinese lyricists explored poetic realms and language we must know a bit about their world and the linguistic resources of their genre. Thus, it is worthwhile to orient readers who want to understand the historical and cultural context in which these poets wrote.

Politically, the seventeenth century was an era of tumult and great change, an era that saw the collapse of a Chinese dynasty and the establishment of an alien dynasty of conquest. Perhaps because it was an age that tried men's souls and shook their faith in the political order, seventeenth-century literati produced a slew of masterpieces in semipopular or neglected genres. Tang Xianzu (1550–1616) crowned the southern tradition of dramatic romance with his *Peony Pavilion*. Unknown novelists created China's greatest erotic novels, *Golden Vase Prunus* and *The Prayer Mat of Flesh*. Feng Menglong (1574–1646) and Ling Mengchu (1580–1644) brought the art of the vernacular story to its culmination, while Pu Songling (1640–1715) recast classical tales of the supernatural into works of a haunting, almost Gothic, strangeness and beauty in his *Strange Tales from Leisure Studio*. In poetry, the *ci,* or "lyric," rose phoenix-like from the ashheap of history, regaining for a time most of its former splendor.[1]

By the early seventeenth century, literati deciding whom, how, and whether to serve as officials faced excruciating problems. The Ming was so autocratic that high officials could be beaten to death at court audiences. Its later rulers were so feckless that, for one period of twenty-five years, no imperial audience was held at all. Ming tyrants even abolished the post of prime minister, resulting in a paralyzing weakness of the executive branch.[2] Accordingly, the bureaucracy was riven by factional strife between an "inner" party of cabinet members and eunuchs and an "outer" party of court officials.[3] Historians have asserted that "at no time in Chinese imperial history were court politics and ethics more debased," and the morale of the literati was low.[4] Although the Ming managed to find servitors even in its death throes, by the 1630s many literati had grown chary of government office.[5]

Domestically, landed Chinese gentry viewed the early seventeenth century as a period of economic decline and social disruption. During the late sixteenth century, a growth in interregional trade and in specialized, commercialized agriculture created a more important role for money. Gentry landowners saw more and more sons of wealthy plebeians crowding the pool of examination candidates, saw their tenants growing increasingly unruly, and saw their own elite status and local authority becoming daily more precarious.[6]

Then, in the early seventeenth century, the depression in Europe and the Americas slowed China's net inflow of silver to a trickle, causing a serious lack of specie and wreaking havoc on specialized commodities growers. Simultaneously, the "little ice age of Louis XIV" burdened China with severe weather and devastating crop failures. By the 1640s, the Chinese rice bowl in Jiangnan (the lower Yangzi region) had become a cauldron of drought, hunger, epidemics, rent strikes, and rebellion.[7] Although the Ming raised tax rates to unbearable levels, too much gentry land remained beyond its grasp. Unable to reform revenue practices to adjust to changing economic conditions, the dynasty, too, was starving for lack of grain and specie.[8]

As luck would have it, just at this time China faced simultaneous challenges on two frontiers. In the northwest, decades of destitution and Muslim unrest had bred armies of peasant rebels. By 1641, the rebel generals Li Zicheng and Zhang Xianzhong had captured the strategic cities of Loyang and Xiangyang, respectively, and stood poised to pounce on the Central Plain and Jiangnan.[9] Northeast beyond the Great Wall, descendants of twelfth-century Jin invaders had captured most of Manchuria, proclaimed the Qing dynasty, and mounted a serious military threat to the nearby Ming capital in Beijing. The once-proud Ming army, more than a million strong, had unraveled to the point of helplessness. The early Ming system of self-sufficient agromilitary garrisons had long since degenerated, replaced by a scandalously expensive and inefficient mercenary army. By 1640, the nearly bankrupt Ming regime was forced to rely on unscrupulous warlords, many of them former bandits. The Ming's doom was sealed when it became unable to feed and equip its armies, while both rebels and Manchus took the lead in utilizing firearms and ordnance.[10] When Beijing and the north fell in 1644, it was hard to say which was more remarkable, the ailing Ming's tenacity or the swiftness of its final collapse.

The reaction of southern literati to this crisis was less than glorious. Many did engage in regional mobilization and rally to support the "Hongguang emperor," a Ming scion who established a rump regime in Nanjing. But the southerners could not convince the Hongguang emperor that their regional defense and restoration were compatible.[11] These southern heirs of the reformist "East Wood" (Donglin) literati lost a nasty internecine squabble with northern warlords and remnants of the "inner" faction. As a result, popular support for the regime eroded, the defense of Jiangnan was crippled, and the Qing invasion force swept south almost unopposed.[12]

After the Qing conquered Jiangnan in 1645, more Ming princes established shaky regimes in the far south (the best known being the "Yongli emperor's" court in the southwest, 1645–1661). All fell victim to a lack of cooperation between princes, to a dearth of popular support, and to infighting between civil officials and the military strongmen in whose hands the southern Ming's fate actually rested. By 1661, the last Ming pretender had been put to death, and the Manchus had completed their astounding con-

quest. During the next twenty-five years, they completed the consolidation of China by regaining political control, accommodating
Chinese interests, restoring social order, and routing rebellious
warlords.[13]

In this process, the Manchus were aided by Chinese literati,
whose commitment to the Ming was far from complete. Indeed,
many southerners had been roused to action, not by the 1644 conquest of Beijing, or even by the 1645 invasion of Jiangnan, but by
the Qing edict ordering Chinese men to shave their heads and
adopt the Manchu queue.[14] This insult to Chinese manhood in-
cited a rash of ill-coordinated and often suicidal mutinies, but
they were too little and too late. Moreover, the gentry's interests
as local leaders and as property owners lay in collaboration with
the Qing, not in a war of restoration.[15] The desperate violence all
about them and their own intense conflicts between Confucian
notions of loyalty and desires to regain local order drove Chinese
literati to a variety of actions.

Some "romantics" continued to indulge in the aestheticism
and sensuality that had characterized the late Ming, fiddling
while Beijing burned and then seeking an accommodation with
the Manchu regime. The most famous example of this type was
the eminent poet, critic, and literary patron Qian Qianyi (1582–
1664). Among the lyricists in this book, Wu Weiye (and, to an
extent, Chen Weisong) fits this pattern. Others adopted a "stoic"
attitude toward the Ming collapse, turning from anti-Qing resistance to the consolations of philosophy and scholarship, maintain-
ing their integrity by refusing to serve the Qing. The most famous
example of this type was the scholar Gu Yanwu (1613–1682); of the
lyricists in this book, Wang Fuzhi (and, to an extent, Zhu Yizun)
best fits this pattern. Finally, a few of the more impetuous scholars
took up arms against the Qing and died martyrs' deaths. Of the
lyricists in this book, only Chen Zilong was forced to pursue such
a course (Nalan Singde also died young, but apparently because
he was a martyr to love, not politics—see below).[16]

The next generation of scholars grew up traumatized by the
horrendous events that had driven their fathers to suicide, collab-

oration, or withdrawal. The sons were troubled by ambivalence toward their ruthless but capable alien conquerors, by dissatisfaction with the culture, intellectual currents, and literary style of the late Ming, and by frustration at the paucity of official posts open to Chinese scholars.[17] When the "Manchu conquest elite" embarked on a "nativist" course in the 1660s, southern Chinese literati suffered many kinds of persecution.[18] For example, nearly fourteen thousand gentry were indicted and many jailed for being in arrears in taxes. One young literatus was so unhinged by his incarceration that, on returning home, he slaughtered his entire family.[19] Other prominent literati were killed by the Qing for protesting the tax case or for writing on topics sensitive to the Manchus.[20] Some more impulsive Chinese began to act like "knights-errant," seeing a romantic appeal in playing Robin Hood to bring justice to a society whose government would not provide it.[21]

Only later in the 1670s did southerners begin to find more opportunities for official service. Meanwhile, many more literati found employment as mandarins' "secretaries" and as scholars in the hire of official patrons. A few poets and scholars even won the favor of the "Kangxi emperor" himself, thanks to the ruler's keen appetite for new knowledge and for a source of support independent from his Manchu regents.[22] Of the poets we shall examine, Chen Weisong fits the type of frustrated office seeker, Zhu Yizun illustrates the special opportunities open to gifted Chinese, and Nalan Singde exemplifies the role that literary patronage played in improving relations between Manchus and Han Chinese.

The possibility of gaining imperial favor through poetry suggests a clue to our central mystery: why did seventeenth-century literati begin writing lyrics in such numbers? By the late Ming, the lyric had languished for three hundred years. The tunes to which lyrics were "filled in" had been lost so that Ming lyricists could fill in words only according to older models. Reliable prosodic manuals had not yet been compiled, and models were scarce; most Soong collections of lyrics were unavailable during the Ming.[23] Writers who preferred popular songs wrote *qu* ("dramatic lyrics"), while classically inclined literati wrote *shi* poetry.

The dominant "Archaist" school of literary theoreticians proclaimed that

> Prose must be of Qin and Han; *shi* must be of High Tang.[24]

Scholars like Li Panlong and Wang Yuanmei even asserted that no poetry written after the High Tang was worth reading.[25] When not even Soong *shi* poetry was deemed worthy of notice, the less prestigious *ci* was bound to suffer neglect. It is hard to imagine what, short of imperial fiat, could have possessed seventeenth-century scholars to have revived this hoary but none-too-respected genre.

Nonetheless, I am forced to conclude that imperial patronage had little to do with the renaissance of lyric poetry. True, the Kangxi emperor (r. 1662–1722) loved a good lyric. He showed special favor to the lyricist You Tong, praised a collection of lyrics by Chen Weisong and Zhu Yizun, and honored Nalan Singde with a position in the imperial bodyguard.[26] Yet all these marks of favor occurred during the late 1670s, when most of the lyrics in this book had already been written. The publication of the *Imperial Registry of Lyric Prosody,* which officially conveyed the dynasty's approval of lyric songs, had to wait until 1715. Thus, imperial favor cannot explain why lyrics flourished in the seventeenth century, although lack of imperial condemnation certainly enabled lyrics to flourish.

The years 1645–1670 were a tense age in which the Manchu regime executed whole clans for sentiments expressed or implied in *shi* poems and essays. As a less prestigious genre not commonly considered a proper medium for "expressing intent," the lyric provided a safer means to vent, however obliquely, sorrow and disgust at the course of contemporary events.

Another possible stimulus to the renaissance of the lyric was political chaos itself. It is widely held that political breakdown can spur artistic creativity by breaking down old paradigms and by forcing poets' thoughts into new molds. Of course, the fall of the Ming and the attendant social changes were not devastating enough to impel traditionalist Chinese poets to relinquish literati ideals. On the contrary, social leveling only made them cling more tightly to their claim to status—their knowledge of old texts. Hence, it seems most appropriate that political upheaval and social chaos would lead Chinese literati to exhume a fossilized popular genre.[27]

At the same time, the lyric was considered a suitable medium for expressing tenderer, less elevated sentiments. Literati who found Ming dramatic lyrics too crude could turn to Soong lyrics, which had a cachet of antiquity and which had become quite respectable during the Soong. Antiquarian Qing scholars were wont to revive Soong habits of thought and styles of literature, if only because they provided an alternative to the "debased" culture of the Yuan and Ming.[28] Although Ming archaists had claimed not to read poetry written after the age of Du Fu, some, notably Wang Yuanmei (1526–1590), were fond of writing in the ornate, sensuous manner of Late Tang poetry.[29] Early lyrics closely resemble the baroque style of poets like Li Shangyin, so it becomes less surprising that an archaist like Wang Yuanmei actually wrote a collection of lyrics himself. During the 1650s, Wang Shizhen (1634–1711), the preeminent poet of his time, became fond of writing lyrics. His example provided an important impetus to the rediscovery of the genre. Ironically, when Wang Shizhen became a high official, he then denounced the lyric as "a trivial art, like carving bugs."[30]

Finally, it is certain that budding lyricists received inspiration from the lips of singing girls and boys, the very groups who first popularized the lyric. Qing critics are fond of lamenting that, since the Soong tunes had been lost, "lyrics from the Ming onward have changed from a matter of music to a [mere] matter of words."[31] Yet, if we abandon the Chinese literatus' antiquarian stance, we will realize that the loss of old music does not preclude the performance of lyrics to new or newer tunes. In fact, there is evidence that higher-class entertainers *did* sing both old and new lyrics to some kind of music (see below).

It is hard to say just which of these factors was the key to reviving the seventeenth-century lyric, and we must be cautious about attributing complex phenomena to a few simple causes. But clearly, in retrospect, a genre that was extant yet untainted by association with the decadent Ming, that was permissible in polite society yet vitalized by musical performance, that appealed both to romantic yearnings and to love for antiquity, was bound to be a hit with seventeenth-century scholars.

Genre of the Lyric

Before we begin our examination of early Qing lyrics, however, it is necessary to know a bit more about the essential features and history of the genre.[32] Lyrics, for our purposes, are song words "filled in" according to tune patterns that determine the number of lines in the poem, the number of syllables in each line, and the alternation of level and oblique tones throughout the poem. Most lyrics are composed of two stanzas, each divided into two or more strophes—that is, into complete sentences ended by a rhyme.[33] The lines within each lyric tend to be of varying length (an exception is given below). Lyrics are of two kinds: the "short tune" *(xiao ling)* of less than sixty-three syllables, whose stanzas tend to be symmetrical and whose strophes roughly correspond to the couplets of modern-style *shi* poetry; and the "adagio" *(man ci)* of more than seventy syllables, whose stanzas are usually asymmetrical and whose strophic structure deviates farther from that of *shi* couplets.[34]

The lyric enjoyed a complex and fascinating evolution in which literati composition, popular performance, foreign music, and court patronage each played a role.[35] As the genre matured during the tenth and eleventh centuries, most literati wrote "short tunes" in the "oblique and concise" style, conveying romantic longings or exploring melancholy, refined sentiments.[36] Others (notably Liu Yong) incorporated elements of folk style and created "adagios" with a greater component of realistic description, frankly expressed emotion, and colloquial diction.[37]

In the late eleventh century, Su Shi shaped the lyric into a vehicle capable of treating a wide range of subjects and moods, from the sublime to the comic, from the sentimental to the philosophical.[33] Meanwhile, Zhou Bangyan created subtle and sophisticated poetic worlds in which the lyricist's voice is submerged by its empathy with objects and engages in complex "metaphorical explorations."[39] The innovations of Su and Zhou essentially determined the further course of the lyric in the southern Soong. Partisans of Su's "literati lyrics," like Xin Qiji, cultivated a "powerful and unrestrained" style as they explored a range of philosophical, heroic, or witty sentiments.[40] Devotees of Zhou's style, like Jiang Kui, escaped into meticulously crafted, "exquisite and rarefied" private realms of emotional and aesthetic experience, often transmuting personal emotions altogether in their "retreat toward the object."[41] Since the lyric experienced no further progress until the seventeenth century, this was the generic heritage that mid-seventeenth-century lyricists enjoyed.

As we explore these lyrics, we will want to keep two central questions in mind. What did the seventeenth-century lyricists contribute to the development of the genre? How do their efforts compare to those by their Soong predecessors? Our answers may not shake the earth, but the patient, open-minded reader will reap some fine verses and some insights that undercut prevailing notions about the vitality of the Chinese lyric tradition.

Chen Zilong

(1608–1647)

The historian John Wills has observed that, at the end of the Ming dynasty, "events were surrounded *as they happened* by dense clouds of role-playing and fabulation; even when one sticks to the best and closest primary sources, the people and events seem almost incredible."[1] The almost legendary character and exploits of Chen Zilong (1608–1647), nicely fueled by Chen's "chronobiography" written by himself and completed by an adoring disciple, bear out Wills' observation. Chen Zilong excelled as scholar, magistrate, poet, officer, and, in his spare time, as lyricist.

Biography

Chen was born into a literati family in Songjiang, heart of the Yangzi Delta's "cotton country." Even Chen's birth is tinged by the uncanny; before delivery, his mother dreamed she saw "a dragon glowing and undulating on the bedroom wall."[2] Thus, Chen was named Zilong, "child-dragon."

Scholastically, Chen Zilong's youth followed a familiar plot: precocious brilliance, early exam success, and an official post before the age of thirty. Chen's father had been a reform bureaucrat associated with the East Wood faction, and Chen joined one of the flourishing Jiangnan study societies. In 1628, Chen helped found another, the Incipient Awareness Society (Ji She). This group espoused neoclassical prose and poetry, following the precepts of the archaist Latter Seven Masters of the Ming.[3]

In the tumultuous last decades of the Ming, study societies and factional politics were inseparable, and Chen Zilong soon became deeply embroiled. When Suzhou rioted in opposition to eunuch Wei Zhongxian in 1626, Chen and some schoolmates actually burned Wei in effigy, a bold prank they were lucky to pull off with impunity. Soon after, Chen embarrassed his study group when he squared off against an older scholar opposed to neoclassicist dogma and, according to some observers, even came to blows over the issue of correct classical models![4]

As his political career advanced, Chen never ceased his involvement in controversial affairs. During his membership in the Restoration Society, Chen wrote frequent criticisms of Ming civil and military institutions. As soon as he earned his "presented scholar" degree, Chen became involved in a factional dispute at the capital. Sidelined by an enforced period of mourning for his stepmother, Chen edited a massive, 504-chapter compilation entitled *Selected Writings on Statecraft during the Ming Period.* In 1640, Chen received his first post as magistrate of a poor county in Shaoxing, Zhejiang. During the next two years, Chen proved so successful at combatting famine, plague, and bandits that he was selected as one of the eight outstanding local officials of the empire.[5] Having become an expert on military strategy, Chen was assigned to quell Zhejiang bandits in 1642, then to bolster fortifications around Hangzhou and Suzhou. When a Zhejiang militia organizer ran afoul of local authorities, Chen defeated the militia, then rode alone into the rebel camp and persuaded the organizer to surrender.[6]

Such exploits could not, however, shore up the collapsing house of Ming. In 1644, Chen reported to the rump government in Nanjing and, amid the fierce factional struggles plaguing the court, continued to speak out on the issues of the day. When much of Jiangnan rebelled against Qing orders to shave their foreheads and adopt the Manchu queue, Chen led a mob into the city of

Songjiang; brandishing a portrait of the Ming founder, Chen had them put the Qing magistrate to death.[7] When the rebellion fizzled, Chen fled to a Buddhist monastery and lay low for a time. In the spring of 1647, he was implicated in another unsuccessful plot against Qing authorities and was captured. Chen's final acts are almost too true to his heroic image to be believed. Chen reportedly refused to submit to his interrogators and, when asked why he had not cut his hair, replied, "I am keeping it, that I may face my sovereign in the world below."[8] Chen was loaded into a small boat bound for trial in Nanjing but leaped into the swift current and drowned himself.[9]

What is missing from Chen Zilong's public chronobiography is any hint of his reason for composing lyrics. One suspects, correctly, that there was a less respectable side to this upright patriot and classical scholar. We do know that, as a young exam candidate who became head of a large household at eighteen and who failed the "presented scholar" exam twice, Chen must have endured enormous pressures in performing his public roles. We read that Chen was a flamboyant, magnanimous host; during the 1630s, his house was thronged with scholars attending "poetry and wine" parties. The expense strained the family budget, and his wife was forced to take economizing measures.[10] Chen's chronobiography also tells us that he had three concubines in his first eleven years of marriage.

But the raciest chapter in Chen's life, the one that holds the key to Chen's fondness for lyrics, has long been suppressed. Why? Because Wang Yun (1619–1693?), Chen's disciple and editor of his chronobiography, was a devoted friend of Chen's wife. Wang wrote a slanderous account of the famous courtesan Liu Rushi and refers to Ms. Liu once in an anecdote at the end of the chronobiography. According to the tale, Ms. Liu attempted to befriend Chen, but Chen repulsed her with "severe uprightness."[11] In Qian Qianyi's memoirs, the tale is embellished to include a retort by Liu: "You don't even know beauty when you see it; how can you be called a 'celebrated literatus?' "[12]

Why did Wang Yun feel compelled to deny a relation between Chen Zilong and Liu Rushi? More than sixty years ago, Luo Zhenyu theorized that Chen and Liu had, in fact, had a liaison. Recently, Chen Yinque has made a strong case for the theory.[13] In his monumental *Account of Liu Rushi,* Chen Yinque displays an indefatigable determination to "uncover the hidden facts" at all costs, reading Ms. Liu's presence and Chen's love into every belle and languishing lover in Chen's oeuvre. Chen Yinque does provide enough evidence, however, to convince us that Chen Zilong and Ms. Liu did have an affair. During a two-year hiatus in Chen's annal, during which, we are laconically told, Chen spent his time "studying" at a friend's estate, the two were probably living together.[14]

Aside from intrinsic interest, this love story is crucial to our understanding of Chen Zilong. Liu Rushi was famous both as a poet and as a singer, and the influence of talented geishas on scholar-lyricists has long been appreciated in China.[15] Though we are assured that almost no Soong music survived into the seventeenth century, there is evidence that *ci* lyrics *were* put to some kind of music, most likely the Kunshan tunes to which Ms. Liu and her ilk sang the popular and art songs of the day.[16] Most of the famous seventeenth-century lyricists and singing girls came from the towns around Suzhou and Hangzhou. Indeed, Ms. Liu's home was Shengze, touted as the home of the finest silk market and songstresses in China.[17] Shengze was located in Jiaxing County, just south of Songjiang.

Even if the relationship between Chen Zilong and Ms. Liu were less intense than Chen Yinque thinks, it is certain that Chen Zilong, with his passionate nature and zest for adventure, was fascinated by the women and songs of Shengze. Though written proof is lacking, I imagine that this less-publicized period of Chen's life explains why he was able and disposed to write such marvelous lyrics. But enough gossip; it is time to hear some of Chen Zilong's "songs."

Poetic Worlds

Tune 1, *Touching Up Carmine Lips (Dian Jiangchun)*
On a Spring Day, Moved by Wind and Rain (XZC, 20.2a)

Spring's glory fills my eyes,
The east wind's wont to blow the pinks away.
How many bouts of mist and fog?
Only the flowers are hard to defend.

In a dream I longed for . . .
That princely road to my old country.
Spring has no master!
Where the cuckoo cries.
Its tears dye rouged rain.

Line 6. Chen implies a wanderer's sorrow by alluding twice to the *Chuci:*

The prince is roving, O and won't come back.
Prince, come back! O You cannot stay long in the hills;
Spring grasses grow, O so lushly!

Line 9. Metamorph of a legendary homesick king of Shu, the cuckoo is supposed to cry, "Best go home!" and to weep tears of blood.

In this lyric, the spring wind stirs up a restless mood. Wind and bad weather whirl away nature's glory and vanquish the helpless flowers. Allusions to the *Chuci* nicely weave the related themes of transience and loss. References to "that princely road to my old country" and to the exiled king of Shu and the exclamation "Spring has no master!" suggest a political dimension to the speaker's helplessness. But the closing returns to the oblique mode and the delicate, evocative imagery characteristic of most Five Dynasties lyrics. The rain, already rouge stained by flowers, takes on a deeper hue from the cuckoo's tears. The strong transitive verb "dyes" joins the feminine flowers and tears of blood in a conceit worthy of Li Shangyin, fusing an image of substitution with a mythical figure to enhance the mood of nostalgic despair.

TUNE 2, *Spring in the Painted Hall (Huatang Chun)*
Apricot Blossoms in the Rain (XZC, 20.5a)

A pondside lodge in slight shadow, a bridge at water level.
  Another bout of flowering branchtips toying with rain.
Where the faint chill touches, so surpassingly sweet.
    It's here the soul is seared.

  I recall long ago beyond Bluegate Causeway,
  Powdery scents whirled wildly every morn.
Jade faces grow lonesome, pale pinks swirl.
    Helpless against tonight.

Line 5. Formerly a city gate of Chang'an, here "Bluegate" denotes any city gate. It also suggests the "Blue Houses" in which Chinese courtesans dwelt. This implication is reinforced by the "powdery scents" and by the phrase "every morn." When the amorous goddess of Witch Mountain proposed to the king of Chu, she promised to make clouds and rain "every morn and even." "Clouds and rain" has become the conventional euphemism for intercourse. Here, the rain that marks spring's passage also betokens that sexual love can hasten the ruin of beauty.

    This lyric, too, displays a concern for "flowers hard to defend." The poet's keen appreciation of their fragile beauty is reminiscent of the Japanese court poet's *aware*.[18] The mood created by "slight," "toying," "flowering branchtips," "faint," "touches," and "sweet" is even more delicate and sensuous than that in the previous poem. The second stanza expatiates on the poet's "soul-seared" response. Whether in memory, in perception, or in anticipation, he sees only the inevitable ruin of beauty. His deft use of the pathetic fallacy, particularly the final displacement of helpless feelings to the "jade faces," lends their fate a special poignance.

TUNE 3, *Song of Mountain Blossoms (Shanhua Zi)*
Springtime Griefs (XZC, 20.6c)

Willow trees blurry mid the morning mist.
Apricot blossoms scattering at the dawn bells.
Beyond a silent Grandlight Palace, the moon
    Shines on fading pinks.

Polychrome robes turned to butterflies, the gold threads gone;
Whitewash powder chewed by beetles, the jade tower vacant.
Only an unfeeling pair of swallows
    Dances in the east wind.

Line 3. "Grandlight Palace" was the home of the Last Ruler of the Chen (r. 583–587). When his kingdom was overrun, his consorts leaped into a well to avoid defilement. The ruler leaped on top of them and so was captured alive.

Line 5. When the king of Song stole Han Ping's wife, Han committed suicide. Han's wife cut the threads of her gown and, when she accompanied the king to a pavilion, threw herself off the parapet. As the king's attendants grabbed at her sleeves, her garments "transformed into a butterfly," and she plunged chastely to her death. Now the poet sees real butterflies cavort before the threadbare ones embroidered on a screen.

In this spring lament, the dominant theme of evanescence is linked to cycles of ruin and decay in the human world. Thanks to the binomes "blurry," "scattering," and "silent," as well as "fading," the tattered embroideries and crumbling walls, "gone," "vacant," and "unfeeling," the lyric maintains a consistently melancholy mood. References to plunging palace ladies and to the vacant tower suggest an elegy for a doomed dynasty. But it is hardly necessary to read the swallows as symbols of disloyal officials.[19] Instead, we may view the faithfully migratory birds just as we view the butterflies and beetles, as emblems of nature's eternally recurring indifference to our particular human woes.

TUNE 4, *River City Song (Jiangcheng Zi;* XZC, 20.15b)
Rising from Sickness: Spring Is Done

A curtainful of sunrise belltolls around my sick-bed.
    Sunrise clouds grow empty.
    Furling up scattered pinks.
The heartless hues of spring have left—
    When shall we meet again?
Even tho' I added a thousand streams of purest tears . . .
    Undetainably gone,
    Deplorably swift.

In palace of Chu and garden of Wu, the weeds do flourish.
    Lingering by a fragrant copse.
    Orbits an errant bee.
I imagine that in years to come I'll meet you
    On painted screens.
I with my broken heart, flowers with their smiles;
    Rely on the swallows
    To curse the east wind!

Here is yet another world that rings with the hollowness of loss. Each stanza is bifurcated into two strophes of description, then two strophes of response. In the first stanza, the sick, sleepless poet describes his present grief for departed spring. In the second stanza, the purview of his griefs expands to include ancient ruins and thoughts of the future. Man and nature are sundered in the last few lines; the disconsolate poet will not risk any more direct confrontations with flowers or springtime breezes. In the whole, mutable world, only the faithful swallows of spring seem to strike a sympathetic note with their chatter.

The second stanza's opening recalls these lines from an elegy Emily Dickinson wrote in a cemetery (her "Opus 813"):

> This Passive Place a Summer's nimble mansion
> Where Bloom and Bees
> Exist an Oriental Circuit
> Then cease, like these—.

But the voice in Dickinson's poem has achieved a quiescent concord with mortality, while Chen's speaker no longer has the heart to rail at the forces of mutability.

TUNE 5, *The Beautiful Lady Yu (Yu Meiren)*
Impressions (XZC, 20.10ab)

Burgeoning peach and ruddy apricot, spring just halfway.
    Ever altered by the perfumed breeze.
The princely road mid fragrant grass grows fainter, indistinct.
Only the blue hills, as before, face the sunset light.

It's as if her gauzy silks were here, yet no one comes.
    The full moon shines in vain . . .
Midst a dream in the upper chamber, water streaming down.
Casting down a skyful of stars and dew on Jiangnan.

This lyric is marked by the polyphonic interplay of diurnal, seasonal, and human time. One voice in the fugue records the passage of day into night, from burgeoning flowers and perfumed breezes, to the setting sun, to the full moon, to dreams and the late night fall of stars and dew. A second strain is Chen's obligatory lament for seasonal change, heard in the aging flowers and overgrown road. But the poem is distinguished by heavy overtones of human events. Chen mourns a lost kingdom with his reference to the errant prince and with line 4, which has a flavor similar to the opening of Du Fu's dirge for the High Tang, *Spring Prospect:*

> The state is smashed, mountains and rivers remain;
> The city turns vernal, grass and trees grow lush.

The second stanza, with its pervasive sense of emptiness and loss, resembles Li Yu's "late" lyrics, like those Li wrote to the tune *The Beautiful Lady Yu.* Line 3 recalls the interrupted dream from the first stanza of Li Yu's *Waves Scouring Sand:*

> Outside the curtain, rain streams down.
> Spring's mood is fading.
> Gauzy covers can't withstand the chill of dawn.
> In a dream I forgot that I'm a sojourner;
> And for a spell I craved for joy.[20]

The last line of Chen's lyric may sound pretty, but its images of fallen stars and chilly dew are ominous. They and the interrupted dream intimate a fall from grace. It is not farfetched to discern in this lover's plaint a Ming loyalist's lament for his vanquished state.

Tune 6, *Butterflies Lingering over Blossoms (Die Lian Hua)*
A Spring Day (XZC, 20.13b)[21]

Yellow dusk beyond the rain, dawn beyond the flowers.
  Hastening on the drifting years;
    This sorrow, when will it end?
The swallows have come again, as spring grows old.
I face the jumbled pinks, with penciled brows in fret.

The noon dream recedes, its homeward route obscured.
  Upon awakening I feel dizzy;
    I've trampled every blade of the idle courtyard's grass.
How many times must the east wind vex my mood?
Deep, deep in the tiny yard, a fragrant heart contracts.

In this lyric, too, the poet's preoccupation with transience and loss weighs heavily. The spatializing images in lines 1 and 2 plunge the speaker into swiftly passing time. Even the sight of spring flowers mirroring her adorned face brings a frown, as she notes the disarray wreaked by rainy days. Stanza 2 finds the speaker even more frustrated. Asleep, dreams of home are elusive; awake, obsessive thoughts leave her hazier still. The closing image of a shrinking "fragrant heart" aptly catches both the vulnerability of spring flowers and the constrained circumstances of the speaker.

The lyrics in Chen Zilong's anthology are identified with the common label "poetic overflow" *(shiyu)*, indicating lighter verses composed when a poet has time and energy left over after pouring out his nobler sentiments in *shi* poetry. The term is apt because the range of poetic worlds in Chen's lyrics is severely limited. Chen reserves poems "expressing intent" *(yan zhi)*, voicing concerns about his career and the fate of the Ming dynasty, for his ancient-style and regulated verse. These verses have been praised for their "nobility of spirit," their "concern for troubled times," and their "genuineness."[22] In most of Chen's quatrains, we find a different sort of poetic world, one filled with languishing ladies, laments about unhappy love, spring outings, and boudoir songs.

These quatrains are pervaded with the hothouse atmosphere of Late Tang poets like Li Shangyin and Yuan Zhen.[23] The worlds in Chen's seventy-nine lyrics are similar and equally limited in range. Most are filled with fading flowers, loneliness, and sorrow for the transience of beauty. In a few lyrics (like the *Beautiful Lady Yu* translated above), the prevailing mood of loss and regret takes on political overtones, as the poet appears to mourn the fall of Jiangnan. But Chen's lyrics remain wholly within the range of tenth-century models like those from the anthology *Among the Flowers*. Compared with the lyrics of, say, Wen Tingyun, Chen does imbue his songs with a more "personal" tone by frequent use of subjective rhetoric. But even more frequently, Chen projects emotions onto objects, whose "impersonal" emotions conform to the "oblique and concise" aesthetic of tenth-century lyric poetry.

Language

In his lyrics, Chen Zilong employs uniformly elegant and "poetic" diction. He rarely uses colloquial or erudite speech, nor does he extend the language of the Chinese lyric by coining new expressions or inventing new images. The most important images in Chen's lyrics are those recurrent figures that resonate with conventionally symbolic associations. The east wind and spring breezes appear in all the translated selections and in a high percentage of his lyric oeuvre. The east wind is nearly always an adversary, embodying the vicissitudes of time and fate that doom all beautiful, living things, for example:

> Helpless against the lightsome madness of the wretched east wind. (XZC, 4b)

> Gauzy robes cannot bear the east wind's dance. (XZC, 12a)

> How many times has the east wind pestered her mood? (XZC, 13b)

Flowers, which also appear in all the translated selections, can usually be seen as symbols for beauty and youth buffeted about by the winds of fate. The fragrant grasses so prominent in Chen's lyrics regularly suggest the heedlessness of spring growth, longing for an absent friend or lover, and distance in time and space. The swallows that flit through several of Chen's lyrics represent those faithfully recurring aspects of nature that resist mutability. They may seem sympathetic to the speaker:

> Rely on the swallows
> To curse the east wind! (XZC, 15b)

Or their cheerful bustle as they build nests may arouse the poet's envy:

> Only an unfeeling pair of swallows
> Dances in the east wind. (XZC, 6c)

Let me stress again that these symbols are all thoroughly conventional and are in no way products of Chen Zilong's creative imagination.

Chen's lyrics are furnished largely with images from garden and boudoir. One particularly common furnishing is the curtain hook, which occurs eight times. Most of the time, curtain hooks carry no special emotional burden, but consider these examples:

> Compare the curtain-hook with a broken heart: both unceasing. (XZC, 14a)

> Blossoms encage faint moonlight, paling the curtain-hook.
> Old griefs precipitously climb into my heart. (XZC, 3a)

In these lines, the hook is associated with the speaker's fretful, "hung-up" mood. Even as a curtain is suspended by its hook all day, so her heart is impaled on uncomfortable thoughts.

Chen employs compound images frequently, though again without notable innovation. His outstanding trope is

> Where the cuckoo cries.
> Its tears dye rouged rain. (XZC, 2a)

Most of Chen's compound images involve a similar blending of transference and substitution to endow insentient objects with sad emotions, for example,

> Where the faint chill touches, so winningly winsome. (XZC, 5a)

> Jumbled pinks face each other, with worried, penciled brows. (XZC, 13b)

A final characteristic of Chen's verbal art is his predilection for destructive imagery. Though his poetic diction is generally restrained and decorous, his miniature bedroom-and-garden worlds are frequently rent by brute force:

> Jade wheels have crushed flat the fragrant grass. (XZC, 3b)

> Drop after drop, dripping to shards as level leas turn green. (XZC, 3b)

> Crying to pieces pale yellows of mist and fog. (XZC, 7b)

> How many bouts of east wind?

> In fading moonlight, pear-blossoms shred. (XZC, 7b)

> Unruly crows cry, severing the moonlight on chill branches. (XZC, 13b)

Conclusion

Chen Zilong's lyrics are often likened to those of the *Among the Flowers* poets.[24] One literary historian, apparently suffering from distorted hindsight, even claims that Chen tried but failed to shake off their influence.[25] Since Chen's lyrics are sparing with "erotic decor" and abundant in subjective rhetoric, my reaction to these critics is, Right century, wrong place. Chen's style resembles that of Feng Yansi (903–960), who was also wont to "lodge a mournful chill midst an exuberant, prettified style."[26] Consider Feng's well-known lyric to the tune *Magpie on a Branch (Que Ta Zhi):*

> Six crooks of the railing, nestled by emerald trees.
> Breeze in the willows lightsomely
> Unfurls all their golden strands.
> Who takes up the inlaid zither, adjusting frets of jade?
> Threading the curtain, a pair of swallows flies away.

> A gazeful of roving silk and falling catkins.
> When pink apricots blossom,
> One spell of April showers.
> Awake from sodden sleep to orioles' unruly chatter.
> Cutting short a fine dream that leaves no trace to seek.[27]

In stanza 1 of Feng's lyric, a woman's song disperses nest-building birds. In stanza 2, birdcalls disperse the heroine's dream of marital bliss. Just as in Chen Zilong's poetry, the poet cleverly manipulates natural images to convey the inevitable passage of spring, youth, beauty, and happiness.

Of course, I do not wish to obscure the substantial stylistic differences between Feng and Chen. Feng is more likely to begin a lyric with forceful rhetoric, while Chen's responses are usually found at the end of a stanza. Feng is more exuberant in his use of "erotic decor," while Chen is more puritan, or at least more reticent, about applying sensual adornments. Finally, Chen tends to conclude by projecting strong feelings onto an object, while Feng is wont to end with a more personal closure, such as the common "no trace left to seek."[28]

The chief difference between the two lyricists is that Feng adapted the lyric to express a literatus' refined and subtle moods, creating a style that commanded wide allegiance among northern Soong poets.[29] Chen merely mimicked this style, so his place in literary history cannot match that of Feng Yansi. Traditional critics have praised Feng's lyrics even while condemning him as an unscrupulous politician.[30] Of Chen Zilong, on the other hand, Wang Shizhen wrote that, "not only do [Chen's] lyrics enhance [our perception of] his character, his character also enhances the value of his lyrics."[31]

Still, Chen does deserve a niche in the history of ci; after all, he was the first major lyricist of the seventeenth century and was arguably the finest lyricist in 350 years. Moreover, his championing of the Five Dynasties style exerted a strong influence on Wu Weiye and Wang Shizhen.[32] Chen was highly praised by Wang Shizhen. Tan Xian (1832–1901), with pardonable enthusiasm, even hailed Chen as "the finest lyric poet since the early Ming."[33] I would not accord Chen such lofty praise, but I do feel that, despite his limited range, Chen did write lyrics of unusual beauty and power.

THREE

Wu Weiye

(1609–1672)

Wu Weiye stands out in the seventeenth century as a scholar-artist of lofty and manifold accomplishments. Wu is best known as a *shi* poet, and his heptasyllabic ballads on topical events rank among the most influential verses of the early Qing.[1] Wu wrote at least three southern-style lyrical dramas *(chuanqi)* that received high praise from literati-critics like Wang Shizhen.[2] Wu is credited with the *Concise Account of Quelling the Bandits (Suikou Jilue),* an account of late Ming rebellions still considered a valuable source by modern historians. Incidentally, its censorship during the Qianlong Literary Inquisition meant that publication of Wu's complete works was suppressed until 1911.[3] Wu was also a landscape artist of some repute, and a dozen of his paintings are cataloged in the *Catalogue of Famous Paintings of Successive Ages.*[4] In his spare time, as it were, Wu also produced ninety-six lyrics whose popularity proved troublesome to him during his lifetime.

Biography

The author of all these endeavors was born into a prominent gentry family in Taicang, Jiangsu, an eastern suburb of Suzhou known for its prosperous farms and talented entertainers.[5] Wu was frail and suffered from chronically weak lungs, which caused some delays in his studies. Still, he advanced swiftly enough to attract the attention of celebrated reform literatus Zhang Pu, whose disciple Wu became at the tender age of thirteen. Only ten years later, Wu won the primus in the 1631 "presented scholar" examination, ahead of his mentor! Wu promptly reaped even greater public admiration when he requested and received permission for leave to return home and marry.[6] Such filial concern to provide his family with an heir is, as we shall see, a dominant trait in Wu's character.

Wu served as tutor in the Imperial Academy and, when his uncle died early in 1644, returned home and purchased the estate whose name provided Wu's sobriquet, "Prunus Hamlet." This proved a timely retreat since the Ming capital fell a few weeks later. Wu was despondent on learning of the last Ming emperor's death and resolved to commit suicide. According to his biography, Wu was dissuaded only when his mother beseeched him to think of his parents' welfare. Wu then reported to the southern Ming court in Nanjing but, disillusioned by its fierce internecine struggles, returned after less than two months to serve his parents as a private citizen.[7] Wu remained out of office for nearly ten years.

According to his chronobiography, until 1654 Wu "shut his door and did not even exchange invitations."[8] Actually, after several years of wary seclusion, Wu began to travel about Jiangnan, renewing friendships with southern literati. After 1650, he even established contacts and exchanged poems with high Qing officials.[9] Wu did decline one nomination for office in 1652 but when renominated the next year failed to demur.[10] At the time, Wu's motives were the focus of much suspicion; even now, they are not entirely clear. Sun Kekuan asserts that Wu succumbed to weakness; just as fear of death had kept him from resisting the Qing a decade before, so lust for public office made Wu compromise his integrity.[11] Frederic Wakeman, however, places Wu's decision within the context of court struggles during the 1650s. At a time when Manchu and Han Chinese fought for influence over the young "Shunzhi emperor," the emperor's desire to shake free of the Manchu princes' influence and his personal fondness for Chinese culture augured well for Chinese interests at court. According to Wakeman, Wu Weiye hoped to enhance southerners' position at court by winning a high post. It was to consolidate southern interests that Wu tried to revive the regional "Reform Society," an attempt that failed due to ideological dissension as well as to Qing suppression of literary societies.[12]

Family considerations, too, certainly affected Wu's decision; his parents tearfully bid him go north and serve. Finally, it is possible that Wu simply did not dare refuse the second nomination. The poetry he had written during his years out of office had made him too well known to remain a hermit, and several literati remarked that Wu was "forced to emerge from the hills."[13] Whatever verdict history may render in this murky case, if we accept Wu's own testimony, it is clear that he took office only with the gravest misgivings. En route to office, he ruefully remarked in a famous couplet:

> I am one of Prince Huai's former cocks and mutts,
> But failing to follow him to Heaven, stayed on earth.[14]

This self-lacerating note of pain and regret for having served two masters dominates the poetry from Wu's last eighteen years of life.

Wu Weiye served as libationer in the Imperial Academy for three years before begging leave to return south and mourn his stepmother. Appropriately enough, during his tenure at the academy, Wu was engaged in compiling an annotated edition of the *Canon on Filial Piety*. Even his detractors will have to admit that Wu's conduct at every critical phase of his life reflects a deep, abiding concern for the welfare of his parents. Even among his lyrics, we can find works celebrating or demonstrating filial sentiments.[15] True, Wu could not aspire to the heroic heights of loyalty ascended by men like Chen Zilong. As one anecdotist observed on describing Wu's abortive suicide attempt in 1644, "As he pondered on the impossibility of remaining both loyal and filial, Wu could only bathe his face in tears."[16]

Soon afterward, the Exam Scandal of 1657 erupted. The exam-

iner for the Nanjing Provincial Examination was accused of
favoritism, and subsequent allegations implicated other officials
in the Imperial Academy. Wu was intimate with the chief defen-
dants and had to part with some of his own property to buy his
way out of trouble.[17] Then, in 1660, Wu was swept up in the
Jiangnan Tax Delinquency Case. The Qing court's Manchu
regents took a hard line on Chinese gentry privilege and determined to curb gentry tax evasion. They levied fines on landowners in arrears, indicted 13,500 people, and even threw many landowners into jail.[18] Wu escaped incarceration but surrendered the
bulk of his remaining property to pay delinquent taxes and
fines.[19] His last years were spent under a cloud of diminished circumstances, opprobrium for having served the Qing, and his own
guilty conscience. As Wakeman observes, Wu's later poetry is
haunted by an "obsessive melancholy" perceptible in poetry written from his return to public life (see the lyric *Congratulating the
Bridegroom* below) to his dying day, when Wu remarked:

> In all my life my lot has been anxiety and dread . . .
> Truly I am the most unfortunate man under Heaven.[20]

Summing up the years of service and retirement in one of his last
lyrics, Wu concluded:

> The last eighteen years have been like a dream;
> A myriad affairs, chill and desolate. (MCJC, 22.5b)

It is ironic that the fame of Wu's romantic lyrics undermined his
eremitic posture and caused him so much grief. On the other
hand, Wu's best poetry grew out of the pain and indignity that he
suffered after reemerging in 1654.[21] As we read the following
lyrics, the reader may weigh in his or her mind the balance
between suffering during life and posthumous fame in literary art.

Poetic Worlds

TUNE 7, *Sand of Silk-Washing Stream (Huanxi Sha)*
Boudoir Feelings (MCJC, 21.3a)

Her tear-runneled cheeks faintly pink, eyes half opened.
Behind his back, swiftly she descends the stair.
She plucks flowers from aloft, revealing her lightsome form.

With care she pokes the brazier, incense whirls and winds.
Delicately she jots on writing paper, ink slants askew.
She's wont to guess at idle affairs, trying to act clever.

This is a worthy specimen of the boudoir poetry that Chinese
literati so often condemned in public but devoured in private. But
while most earlier erotic songs involve sad, lonely ladies languishing in their little towers, Wu's is more sprightly. The heroine does
awaken tearfully,[22] but soon she picks up her spirits, skips grace-
fully out the door, and plucks flowers in the garden. Whether stirring up the brazier, playing with an inkbrush, or engaging the
man with chatter, she is convincingly coy and kittenish. Wu's
frivolous tone and dramatist's eye recall Li Yu's famous lyric to
the tune *A Casket of Pearls*.[23]

TUNE 8, *Immortal by the River (Linjiang Xian)*
Encountering an Old Flame (MCJC, 21.5b)

Rambling about on river and lake, ever laden with wine;
    After ten years, again I see Cloud Blossom.
Lithe and lovely as ever, light upon your palm.
        With barely a smile before the lamp, she
        Furtively looses her skirt of shiny gauze.

Your hard-hearted Master Xiao is now haggard and worn;
    In this life I'll always let you down, dear.
On the city wall of Suzhou, the moon at yellow dusk.
        The man at her green window has gone;
        Tears on rouged powder fall willy-nilly.

Line 2. "Cloud Blossom," originally a kind of blue-tinged mica, is a conventional name for a courtesan, just as "Master Xiao" is a conventional name for a young dandy.[24]

Line 3. This refers to Zhao "Flying Swallow," a consort of the Han who, according to legend, was so petite that she could dance on the palm of the emperor's hand.

Line 9. "Green window" is a conventional toponym for a courtesan's room.[25]

Wu Weiye's dramatic talents reappear in this poignant, coherent encounter between old lovers. The "antihero" bears a close resemblance to the speaker in Du Mu's "Easing My Heart," on which Wu's lyric is partly an allusive variation:

> Rambling about on river and lake, carrying a freight of wine;
> Slim Chu waists broke their hearts, dancing light in my hand.
> After ten years I first awaken from my dreams of Yangzhou,
> Having won a name as "hard-hearted rake of the blue houses."

Line 2. According to Chinese legend, a king of Chu was so enamored of slim waists that most of his palace ladies starved to death. The "blue houses," like the "green window" above, signify courtesans' residences.

Both poems are written in a frank, none-too-elegant manner. Wu Weiye surpasses Du Mu in his vivid characterizations of Cloud Blossom, so quick to love and to be hurt, and of the dramatic speaker, a peculiar blend of callousness and affectionate compassion. The closure expresses pity for woman and wastrel alike since both miss the man they once hoped him to be.

TUNE 9, *A Riverful of Red (Manjiang Hong)*
Contemplating the Past at Garlic Hill (MCJC, 22.11b)

Buying wine in Southern Xu,
I listen to
    night rain resound on the Yangzi for a thousand feet.
Recall the year when

Laddie-boy descended east;
Bodhi-bobcat penetrated deep.
A pale-faced bookworm, what could he do?
Yet Master Xiao in kilt and clogs slighted the enemy.
Laughing:
free-spirited in the North Garrison, fond of talking strategy
        With the staff officer.

                Human affairs have changed,
                The wintry clouds are white.
                Ancient battlements in ruins,
                Altar crows are gathering.
All is
        Sand-buried, wave-washed;
        Broken spears, ruined lances.
In the setting sun, tall galleons struck the iron chain;
The west wind blew down every palace of prince and marquis.
Abandoned to:
yellow reeds and bitter bamboos cuffed by the chilly tide,
        Flutes of woodman and fisher.

Title. "Garlic Hill" stands in modern Dantu, Jiangsu, an area also called "Southern Xu."

Line 3. "Laddie-boy" refers to Wang Jun (206–285), who descended the Yangzi from Shu to attack Wu in A.D. 280. When Wu blocked Wang's path with a massive iron chain, he had the links melted with long, hemp-oil torches and then broke through.[26]

Line 4. "Bodhi-bobcat" refers to Tuoba Tao, grand martial emperor of the Northern Wei dynasty (r. 424–451). He once invaded the Song dynasty, reaching the Yangzi near Dantu. Centuries later, it was said that crows still gathered around his shrine there.

Line 6. Here, "Master Xiao" refers to Xie Xuan (343–388), aristocrat-general of the eastern Jin. Xie and the North Garrison Army of his aide, Liu Laozhi, won a gallant battle against alien invaders at Feishui in 383.

This adagio about time and history belongs in the tradition of Su Shi's *Charms of Niannu* and Xin Qiji's *Joy of Eternal Union.*[27] Wu's lyric, too, is structured by oppositions between cosmic, natural time and the human, historical perspective. The little boat where our poet sits drinking is contrasted with the descent of warships and discussions of strategy. Invading armies and regal palaces turn to broken spears and ruined forts. The clash of galleons and winds of war yield to the thrashing tide and whistling flutes.

It is revealing to compare relations between self and past in the three lyrics of Su, Xin, and Wu. The speaker in *Charms of Niannu* contrasts himself with the "free-flowing" figures of history but ends by bridging the gulf with a final libation to the Yangzi moon. *Joy of Eternal Union* portrays

> All the free-flowing spirits
> Lashed by rain and blown away by wind.

Xin piles up classical examples to depict his personal past, then concludes with fears that no one will employ a hale old hero. Wu's speaker is the quietest of the three, intent on communion with the ancient past. He hears it in the laughter of Xie Xuan, the caw of crows at Tuoba Tao's shrine, and the clang of hulls against iron chains. Wu's imaginative reconstruction of the past affords him a privileged perspective close to nature's. As the lyric ends, he hears fishermen's flutes that play now just as then or a thousand years before.

While rivers are commonly seen as symbols of flux, for all three lyricists the Yangzi, or "Endless River," becomes a symbol of cosmic time.[28] Xin, for example, opens his poem:

> Rivers and mountains for a thousand ages.

For Wu Weiye, the river is an elegiac avenue to the past along which the night rain, west wind, and chilly tide carry him back to the Six Dynasties. Of course, for seventeenth-century literati, it was no large journey to leap back and apply the poem topically, substituting "southern Ming" for "southern Dynasties."

TUNE 10, *Congratulating the Bridegroom (He Xinlang)*
In Sickness, Moved to Write (MCJC, 22.7a)

A myriad troubles hasten grizzled hair.
Consider:
    Scholar Gong, who did cut short his natural years;
      Hard to erase his lofty name.
    Hard to treat my ail with physic or herbs;
      The blazing of hot blood in my breast.
    Until you sprinkle it to the west wind and waning moon.
    Gouge out heart and liver, now place them on the ground,
And ask
    Hua Tuo to ease my thousand-knotted bowels.
        Recalling past griefs,
        Redoubles my sad sobs.

My old friends, impassioned, showed a rare integrity.
But over
    those years I still brood, without cease:
      How I lived stealthily amid the weeds.
    Burn moxa between my brows, purge my nose with gourd-
stalks;
      By now, it will be hard to cure.
    Pains I suffered long ago return a thousand-fold.
    To cast off wife and kids like sandals is no easy matter;
In the end
    I'm worthless! Why even say it?
        Mankind's problems,
        How many ever solved?

Line 2. Gong Sheng (68 B.C.–A.D. 11) refused to serve under Han usurper Wang Mang and starved himself to death at the age of seventy-eight.

Line 8. Hua Tuo (fl. 220) was the Chinese Aesculapius.

Line 14. Iron-club Mai (fl. 590) declared he would rather die like a hero than try to cure his jaundice with moxibustion and gourdstalks "and die in bed surrounded by boys and girls."

Line 17. In the "Treatise on Sacrifices to Heaven and Earth," the martial thearch of Han (r. 140–87 B.C.) sighed, "If I could be like the Yellow Thearch, I would see dismissing wife and kids as merely casting off my sandals."[29]

This lyric is widely considered Wu Weiye's magnum opus. Wu creates a compelling illusion that he is pouring out his troubles right in front of us. He achieves this first by objectifying his moral conflict as a medical disorder. Then he makes the disorder more visceral with the hyperbolic "blazing blood," severed entrails, and gourdstalks up the nose. Yet even more effective is Wu's prosy, simple delivery, with its multiple repetitions. Three occurrences of *shi* ("troubles," "matters," and "problems"), three of "hard to" (and one of "no easy . . ."), two of "year," two of "now," and two of "thousand" ("thousand-knotted bowels," "thousand-fold pains") convey the long accretion of sorrow and pain. The last line plays on a close homophone (the homophone is actually a variant in one text) to suggest

> Mankind's problems,
> How many [alternations of] full and waning?

It is a testimonial to Wu's flair for melodrama that traditional critics believed this to be Wu's "deathbed poem"; presumably, they felt the impact of a lifetime's anguish behind it. Unfortunately, this lyric is mentioned in a memoir written by Wu's friend, Tan Xiao, who died in 1657.[30] Still, it is reasonable to read the lyric as an eloquent expression of Wu's chagrin at having been forced to serve the Qing, of a remorse that consumed his last eighteen years of life.

> TUNE II, *Song of Fresh Hawthorns (Shanzha Zi)*
> Thoughts While Traveling (MCJC, 21.2b–3a)

> A foot high, hills beyond the Yangzi;
> A myriad stipples, trees along the Huai.
> Over the rocks, water splashes and streams,
> Flowing away into Blue Brook.

In the sixth month, the north wind is chill;
Falling leaves, morning and night.
I pass through shade and thread the mists;
The woods blacken, the traveler looks back.

This travel poem traces a world like the scroll painting of a sylvan journey. The first strophe is consciously painterly, depicting a distant landscape where hills are reduced to inches and thousands of tall trees to so many dots of ink. The mood of the second strophe is livelier and more intimate, complementing wooded mountains with flowing water (the reader will, no doubt, recall that the Chinese compound for "landscape" is "hills-water").

As the journey wears on, we pass into shadows where the north wind and falling leaves spell an early end for summer. Mention of evening deepens our sense of fading light. In the black forest at the "end" of the scroll, the eeriness of the woods and the traveler's anxiety about where to stay at night induce an involuntary glance over his shoulder. This lyric is more suspenseful than a sackful of Chinese ghost stories. Just where most tales of the supernatural would let the cat out of the bag by conjuring up a ghost, Wu's poem ends, leaving us in the dark about what lies behind the traveler.

TUNE 12, *Immortal at the River*
Visiting Jiading, I'm Moved to Recall Hou Yande (MCJC, 21.5b)

Bitter bamboo plaits a fence, thatch covers the tiles;
   Sea-fields, long abandoned, now tilled anew.
On meeting, still we speak of a twenty-year-old war.
    A chilly tide dashes battle-bones;
    Wild-fires rouse the empty town.

Though the gates are crumbling, guests remain;
   Mournfully, we offer up wine to Scholar Hou.
Again the west wind rises, I can't control my feelings.
    One rhapsody "Longing for an Old Friend,"
    For my old land, and for rootless fame.

Title. Hou Han (or Hou Hong, 1620–1664) was the nephew of Jiading martyr Hou Dongzeng. Hou Han served the Qing and, like Wu Weiye, retired after being implicated in a scandal.

Line 7. Here, I adopt the variant "offer" *(shi)* for "poem" *(shi).* See Zhang (1983, 372).

Line 9. Xiang Xiu (fl. 250) wrote this rhapsody for his deceased friends Xi Kang and Lu An.

It was a Jiading Hou who led an uprising against Qing city authorities, provoking a reprisal that resulted in the slaughter of the entire city on 8 August 1645.[31] Twenty years later, Jiading's scars still appear fresh to Wu Weiye. Hou Han had been known as a popular host and raconteur,[32] and family guests still seem to linger in recollection of his hospitality. But Wu's lyric is not only an elegy for his deceased friend; it is also a requiem for the "old country" now vanquished and a lament for vagaries of fate that saddled Hou's and Wu's names with undeserved scandal.

Compared with the poetic worlds in Chen Zilong's oeuvre, those in Wu Weiye's lyrics exhibit considerably greater variety. Wu, too, explores the well-trodden ways of boudoir poetry, evincing a greater appetite for sensual pleasure and a keener eye for romantic drama than does Chen. Particularly in his adagios, Wu also expresses the private griefs of a meek literatus surviving an age of heroes. Whether Wu contrasts the present with bygone valorous eras (as in *A Riverful of Red*) or conveys a more personal remorse (as in *Congratulating the Bridegroom*), this serious aspect of his oeuvre is very much a "literature of scars." Traces of a consistent personal voice underlie both segments of Wu's work. Whether singing of love or of politics, many of Wu's lyrics are characterized by a world-weary air of "old age's decline."[33] The most common binome in Wu's lyrics is "haggard and worn," which occurs eight times (see esp. MCJC, 21.5b). Many of Wu's adagios end up with conclusions like these:

Tonight I face the traveler before a guttering lamp, feelings haggard and worn. (MCJC, 22.4a).

> Who asks after Rocky Tor's battle-bones?
> In the autumn wind, old trees surround us. (MCJC, 22.4a)

Line 1. Rocky Tor (near Dong'e, Shandong) lay in the path of Qing armies invading south in 1645.

Line 2. "Surround" may also be construed "grown thick around as my waist." Wu is playing on words to convey a martial motif.

Language

Wu Weiye is not known for innovative verbal artistry. Even his most famous heptasyllabic ballads recall the simple, rather trite style of Bai Juyi, gussied up a bit with allusions and dainty imagery.[34] The language of Wu's lyrics is, if anything, more hackneyed, and striking verbal effects are uncommon.

This is not to suggest that Wu's lyrics are bereft of adornment. Most of his shorter songs are decorated, even festooned, with the conventional trappings of boudoir poetry. When describing embroidery, for example, Wu waxes baroque, wielding such intriguing (though thoroughly imitative) tropes as "cloudy brocade," "icy cocoons," "misty pongee," and "purling dragons" (MCJC, 21.1b). Wu describes erotic decor and feminine charms with relish. "Languid eyes" occur a few times in his lyrics (e.g., MCJC, 21.4b), and Wu is especially fond of "pupils" and "wrists," which each occur four or five times, for example:

> Starry pupils beneath the bed-curtains;
> Snowy wrists before the casement. (MCJC, 21.4a)

But Wu is most carried away by dainty, bound feet. References to "gauze stockings" (21.6a), "brocade-patterned pumps" (21.3a), and "high-heeled clogs with Jade-terrace lotus blossoms" (21.1b) stud his boudoir poetry. References to men's sandals and clogs,

too, occur at least nine times. It is not my aim to psychoanalyze
Wu or to overstress his foot fetishism, yet his pedal imagery leaves
indelible stylistic imprints.

Wu's use of compound imagery is sparing and unremarkable.
His more frivolous boudoir songs and "odes on objects" do
employ the occasional pathetic fallacy. Here is a notably humor-
ous example from Wu's ode on the "bamboo wife," a hollow, per-
forated bamboo bolster designed to keep a sleeper cool:

> Enticed by men, she's tossed and tumbled.
> But having no bowels
> Her belly's all the more "free-flowing." (MCJC, 21.4b)

Line 3. In Chinese, "free-flowing" carries the connotation "romantic."

In his longer, more somber lyrics, Wu sometimes employs transference to dramatize the actions of nature and time. Most common is an image of the tide lashing at ancient ruins, for example,

> Sunset rain pelts;
> Chilly tides lash.
> A gray rat scuttles;
> Palace gates collapse. (MCJC, 22.2a)

> Year after year let
> pelting rain lash ruined stelae
> That boys can recognize. (MCJC, 22.1b; cf. 22.3a above)

Wu's lyrics, like his *shi* poetry, are quite allusive. "Chilly tides
lash" is derived from Liu Yuxi's "Stone City Wall":

> Hills surround the ancient state, its circular course intact;
> The tide lashes the empty city wall and silently returns.
> By the Huai River's eastern edge, the moon of former times
> Deep at night comes back across the parapet.[35]

In his shorter lyrics, Wu often quotes from Late Tang poets like
Du Mu (for an example, see MCJC, 21.5b), a practice much in

vogue among lyricists. In fact, nearly all Wu's allusions are references to lines of verse. One he especially liked to rework is Chen
Yuyi's famous:

Tidings of apricot blossoms mid the rain's sound.[36]

Wu's own lyrics include "tidings of early prunus blossoms"
(MCJC, 21.6a, 22.3a) and "Idly I listen for tidings of the yellow
flowers" (MCJC, 22.4a).

A last characteristic of Wu Weiye's poetic language is his prosodic carelessness. Wu is famous for his cavalier attitude toward
rhyme classes.[37] One critic even waggishly suggested that Wu's
unorthodox rhyming stems from his decision as a loyal Ming subject to adhere to the idiosyncratic rubrics of a rhymebook
published during the reign of the Ming's Grand Progenitor![38]
Fortunately, Wu's erratic prosody does not detract from our
enjoyment of his lyrics, though it may well have irked seventeenth-century Chinese readers.

Conclusion

We might compare Wu's short songs to any of those from the
anthology *Among the Flowers*. Wu's love lyrics, however, while
equally focused on sensory experience, are not as lush as most of
the *Flowers* poems. Rather, Wu's frank tone and inclusion of dis-
cursive elements recall the lyrics of Wei Zhuang. Wei, too, is
known for incorporating elements of narration and drama into his
songs.[39] The kinship extends beyond lyrics, for Wei, too, endured
harrowing political upheavals and wrote about them in the
famous ballad "Lament of a Lady from Qin."[40]

Of course, Wu Weiye's adagios owe nothing to Wei Zhuang.
Since Wu's longer lyrics were very popular and were written in
none too elegant a style, they have been compared to the lyrics of
Liu Yong.[41] But, though Wu shares Liu's knack for narration,
Wu did not make important formal innovations or enliven his

lyrics with plain speech to the extent that Liu Yong did. Wu's large-scale meditations on history and personal experience rather resemble literati lyrics in the tradition of Su Shi and Xin Qiji.

To conclude, Wu's lyrics present much greater variety than those of Chen Zilong. In his exploration of lyrical language, however, Wu discovered even less than did Chen. I must concur with Wang Jiyou's criticism that, since Wu never completely mastered the peculiar language of lyric poetry, he was unable to advance its verbal art.[42] Yet Wu was a man whose every pore exuded artistry; even the "poetic overflow" from this painter, poet, playwright, and historian looms large in the history of seventeenth-century Chinese lyrics. Thus, Zhang Xiangling, with pardonable exaggeration, could laud Wu as "the leader of early Qing lyricists."[43]

Wang Fuzhi

(1619–1692)

Some readers will be surprised to hear Wang Fuzhi's name mentioned in connection with lyric verse. After all, Wang is famous for his philosophy, scholarship, and patriotism, not for his poetry. Wang is widely held to be the most profound philosopher of the seventeenth century. His thought is characterized by "materialist skepticism" and by an "evolutionist" view of historical change.[1] Wang's emphasis on concrete situations, his relation of morality to changing circumstances, and his ardent nationalism have made him the favorite premodern philosopher of Chinese Marxist intellectuals.[2]

Wang Fuzhi is also known as a scholar of rare breadth, industry, and originality. His more than seventy works in 358 chapters include studies of nearly every major text in the Chinese classical curriculum. He produced philological studies on all the Four Books and Five Canons. Unsurprisingly, given Wang's preoccupation with changing circumstances and historical relativism, his most influential research involved the *Canon of Changes* and the *Spring and Autumn Annals*. Despite his rejection of Daoist and Buddhist worldviews, however, Wang was broad-minded enough to learn from heterodox thinkers and produced important studies of the *Zhuangzi* and the *Laozi*. Wang even wrote an appraisal of the Buddhist Dharmalaksana ("dharma-nature in all phenomena") sect. Wang's pioneering insights into this "realistic" sect—which "aims at the discovery of ultimate entity of cosmic existence in contemplation, through investigation into the specific characteristics of all existence"—amazed Qing scholar Liang Qichao with their sophistication.[3] Wang has also earned high praise as a historian; his *Appraisal upon Reading the "Comprehensive Mirror"* and *Appraisals of the Soong Dynasty* are masterly and full of fresh insights.[4]

Wang Fuzhi also found time to criticize and write literary works. He is better known for his poetic criticism, which has been hailed for its insistence on the inseparability of "scene" and "emotion," its stress on the primacy of "mood" and "momentum," and its avoidance of dogmatism.[5] Wang also created a play entitled *The Dragon-boat Encounter* and several volumes of verse. Wang's *shi* poetry is typified by patriotic laments about the fall of the Ming dynasty, couched in a style that is highly allusive and even recondite. Without annotations, Wang's *shi* are tough going, and their author's intent is often subtle and difficult to discern.[6] Wang also wrote 279 lyrics; until quite recently, these were the most completely and most undeservedly neglected of his literary efforts.[7]

Biography

Wang Fuzhi (1619–1692) was born and raised in Hengyang, Hunan, just south of China's Southern Marchmount. His family came from military stock and were only fringe members of gentry society until Wang's father, Wang Chaopin (1570–1647), passed the "presented scholar" examinations of 1615 *and* 1621.[8] Wang Chaopin's third son Fuzhi was the most precocious and passed his "provincial" examination in 1642. The next spring, Wang Fuzhi set out for Beijing to take the "presented scholar" exam. Unfortunately for his chances at official advancement, however, the Ming dynasty was just then falling to pieces. Bandits and rebels were swarming over the country. Wang got no further than Nanchang, Jiangxi, before he had to retreat home.[9]

Even Hengyang proved to be no safe haven. The following year, Zhang Xianzhong's horde overran Hunan and summoned literati to serve Zhang. Wang fled to the hills, in his first of many refusals to serve any regime but the Ming, but his father was captured and held hostage. According to the tale in his chronobiography, Wang then lacerated himself, applied poison to the wounds, and had himself carried to Zhang's camp to be exchanged for his father's freedom.[10] The stratagem was apparently successful, for both father and son were released. They fled into the Heng Mountains, where they built a "Lodge for Continuing the Dream," referring to their wish that Ming rule might somehow be restored.

Unfortunately, conditions in Hunan and throughout the empire went from bad to worse, and the Wangs spent most of the next three years on the run from bandits and the Qing invasion force. Wang Fuzhi lost his first wife and then, in the fall and winter of 1647, his second eldest brother, an uncle who had taught him how to write poetry, and his father.[11] Qing forces were experiencing difficulty in pacifying the south, however. When a Jiangxi official rebelled in 1648, Qing control was disrupted by an epidemic of local uprisings.[12] Wang Fuzhi helped lead one of the mutinies in Hengyang during the winter of 1648. When it failed, he fled to Guangdong to advise the refugee court of Prince Gui, the "Yongli emperor" of the southern Ming. As Wang became embroiled in its murky, suicidal factional struggles, he learned that Prince Gui's court was that of a "pretender" in more than one sense, for it observed no more than a pretense of imperial protocol or farsighted policy.[13] In 1650, Wang was sentenced to death for his outspoken views; after his rescue by a sympathetic warlord, he headed back to Hunan. His mother died en route.[14]

Wang was never to leave Hunan again. In 1652, he built a hut on Ginger Hill, another peak of the Heng Mountains. When Qing forces routed southern Ming defenders of Hunan in 1654, he was forced to flee again. For a time, Wang even hid in a cave occupied by Yao aborigines and adopted a Yao alias.[15] As a Ming loyalist and insurrectionist who had refused to take the Qing tonsure, Wang Fuzhi was a marked man. Only in the winter of 1656 was he able to make his way back to Heng Mountain and reinhabit the "Lodge for Continuing the Dream." In 1660, Wang built another lodge, the "Ruined Leaves Hut," only a few miles away. Finally, in 1669, Wang moved to the "Abode for Observing Life" atop nearby Stone-boat Hill, whence derives Wang's sobriquet, "Master Boat-hill."[16]

For the next thirty-two years, Wang buried himself deep in the hills and continued to perfect the remarkable, incisive scholarship he had somehow never forsaken during the years of tumult. In 1678, Wu Sangui, betrayer of two dynasties, summoned Wang to serve his feudatory; Wang refused and fled deeper into the mountains, emerging only when Wu's rabble had been driven from Hengyang.[17] Meanwhile, a steady stream of political, historical, lyrical, philological, and philosophical writings poured forth from Wang's studio on Stone-boat Hill. Though Master Boat-hill himself was frail and suffered from a chronic, wasting illness during his last several years of life, he never stopped studying, chanting, and scribbling until his death at the age of 72.[18]

Wang's biographies give the impression that he was stern, fiery, and indomitable. His character seems to have been rather volcanic. His youth is marked by impetuous engagements in politics, like his membership in a local Hunan reform society in 1640, his 1644 sally into Zhang Xianzhong's camp, his involvement in the 1648 Hengyang mutiny, and his stormy tenure in the southern Ming court.[19] Later, Wang's ardor to emulate Qu Yuan seems to have cooled, and he adopted a stoicism as adamant as igneous rock. Beneath this stony impassivity, however, pain and grief at the Ming's collapse and at the deaths in his family must still have seethed. Wang remained a fiery "philosophe engagé," whose writings retain a passionate moral commitment to "relevant action" and to "realistic pragmatism."[20] The couplet hanging in Wang's studio read:

> The Six Canons exhort me to open up new ground;
> My seven-*chi* frame begs heaven to bury me alive.[21]

Wang's willingness to endure a lifelong interment on Stone-boat Hill and to remain "the last Ming loyalist" demonstrates a moral courage even greater than that of overt Ming martyrs.[22] In this century, his writings, which had lain dormant for so long, helped precipitate the eruption of a nationalist, revolutionary fervor that toppled not only the Qing dynasty but imperial rule itself.

Poetic Worlds

TUNE 13, *Butterflies Linger over Flowers (XXYC,* 10a)
On Goddess Mountain's Bobbing Kohl: "Straining my eyes across the lake's light toward Goddess Mountain, I saw a swathe of green lotus-plants floating on glassy reflections. From here the water passes from Grotto Court [Dongting] Lake and merges with the Yangzi. There it becomes the river of which Xie Tiao wrote:

> The endless Yangzi flows day and night;
> A traveler's heart laments without end.

Of all Hunan's surpassingly fresh sites, this is the culmination!"

In distance vast a little skiff, all heaven in an eye-blink.
     As I strain my eyes across the pure void,
       The cloud's very roots seem to approach.
Slivered reflections haphazardly bob or disappear.
On a crystalline surface spotless hangs her green conch mark.

I recall that ever since the Qin emperor came to visit.
     Yao's daughters, wreathed in frowns,
       Orchid-girdled, have mourned wild will-o-the-wisps.
A thousand tear-stained bamboo-stalks droop in purple nimbus.
But traveling geese bring no message from Cangwu.

Line 5. This is a conventional image of substitution for a woman's "conch-like" coiffure, used here to describe the peak of Goddess Mountain.

Line 7. On his southern excursion, the megalomaniac first emperor of Qin was hindered by a storm on Grotto Court Lake. On learning that the Xiang goddess was responsible, he became enraged and had three thousand convicts lop down all the trees on her sacred mountain, then paint it (convict-)red.[23] According to a later account, the Qin emperor also burned the Xiang goddess' shrine on Goddess Mountain.[24] Yao's daughters, who were given in marriage to Shun the Sage Ruler, are the Xiang goddesses.[25]

Line 10. In legend, Cangwu is the location of Shun's tomb. When he died, Yao's daughters searched, weeping, for his corpse. Their tears supposedly stained the spotted bamboos for which Hunan is famous.[26]

This lyric almost enables readers to shake off mortal dust and espy a celestial world. In reflections between lake and sky, at the limits of vision, we may hope to glimpse the goddess. But such privilege has its price; as in the *Nine Songs* of Chu, a deity's visit ends in letdown. Intrusive memories warn the speaker that even denizens of heaven are vulnerable to the armies of a northern tyrant. As they sacrifice baubles to a will-o-the-wisp (or "ghost fire," an emblem of the dead to Chinese), weep for their lord (Shun), and wait for a message (that will never arrive), the Xiang goddesses are pathetically forlorn. Given Wang Fuzhi's political views, it is nearly irresistible to see this lyric as a lament for a lost kingdom. Hated northern invaders have violated the native goddesses; the poet waits anxiously for news from the south, where lie Shun's grave and the Yongli emperor's refugee court.

Stylistically, *Butterflies Linger over Flowers* offers striking similarities to the *ci* of Jiang Kui (ca. 1155–1221). First, to include an extended preface like Wang's was Jiang Kui's innovation. The preface's lyrical description sets a scene and establishes a mood for the poetic act to follow.[27] Second, Wang's narrator has stepped back so far from the lyric's dramatic center that he does nothing but see and recall. This accords with the "retreat toward the object" that so distinguishes Jiang Kui's aesthetics.[28] Finally, Jiang Kui's style has been characterized as "pure and spare" *(qing kong),* as "clandestine and chilly," and as marked by an individual mode of sensuousness that is lofty rather than vulgar.[29]

"Pure and spare," which occur as "pure void" in Wang's lyric, could well describe the world within *Butterflies;* "clandestinely chill" explicates its mood. Wang's description of Goddess Mountain is certainly free enough of vulgarity, yet it makes a strong appeal to the senses. "Clouds' roots" (a conventional epithet for mountains), "slivered reflections," and "green conch" (kenning for a beehive hairdo) are all quite striking. Still more arresting is Wang's skillful deployment of ocular imagery. The topic of *Butterflies* is a mountain's "mascaraed brows," and this motif persists in "strain my eyes," "wreathed in frowns," and "tear-stained bamboos." Even the basic sense of *shun,* originally "in the blink of an eye," is revived in line 1. *Shun* is homophonous with Shun, the deceased emperor whose epithet is "double-pupiled," creating a subtle link between the opening and closure of *Butterflies.*

TUNE 14, *Song of Groping for Fish (Mo Yuer)*
The Peach Waves of Eastern Islet (XXYC, 2a)

Shearing mid-channel,
White duckweed and fragrant grasses,
The swallow-tailed river parts the southern reach.
Brimmingly bright, ready to mimic spring-blossom dimples;
Girlish faces the same year after year.
Hold spring back!
Laugh at
so much floating cress,
Old dreams straying midst strewn catkins.
Crabapple oars without number.
Drift through
all the moonlit lotuses unfurled,
Hold fast their sylphen skirts,
And go back, laden with spring.

Beauteous, flourishing site;
Sylph Hall far off midst fog and mist.
Drenched scents fly up to vermilion doors.
Over the altar, pearly Dipper shines like scattered lamps;
Together they fill the sky with raining petals.
Don't you complain!
Don't you see:
Peach roots now lost to the Jiangnan crossing.

The wind is wild, the rain jealous.
Even with
    a myriad flecks of fallen blossoms,
    How many bays of flowing water?
    This is not the route for fleeing Qin!

Line 5. These lines describing peach blossoms involve a stock reference to a poem by Cui Hu (fl. 785–805). He was served water by a pretty country lass but had to hasten back to the capital on business. When Cui looked for her the next year, she was nowhere to be found. Cui inscribed a quatrain on the doors of her house:

> Last year upon this day, in this very gate;
> A girl's face and peach blossoms shone each other pink.
> But now the girl's face, where has it gone?
> Peach blossoms, as of old, laugh in the spring breeze.

Line 17. During the reign of the martial emperor of the Liang (r. 502–549), a monk preached the Scriptures so movingly that heaven rained down flowers on the altar. "Raining Petal Terrace" was then built on the site, in Nanjing.

Line 20. Wang Xianzhi (344–386) had two concubines, Peach Root and Peach Leaf. The song he sang on parting from them became so famous that the site was named Peach Leaf Ford, which is also in Nanjing.

The world emerging from this lyric is complex and subtle. On the surface, it describes a famous sight from the Xiao and Xiang region, peach trees on a river islet that, seen from a distance, resembles waves of flowers. As the poet watches catkins fall on the water and turn to cress (an old Chinese folk belief), he longs to hold the springtime back. The "moonlit lotuses" recall the lotus-leaf boat on which the immortal Taiyi sailed, while the reference to "sylphen skirts" reveals a desire to glimpse again the Xiang goddess.[30]

At the beginning of stanza 2, the poet appears to approach that celestial realm, but the happy reverie is snapped by sharp interjections in lines 6 and 7. Whether we interpret "peach roots" literally as islet trees engulfed by spring floods or as a beautiful woman's name, the next line conveys regret for the loss of beauty. The closing laments that, unlike the fortunate denizens of Tao

Qian's "Peach Blossom Source," the Xiang goddesses can find no haven from the invading armies of Qin. The poem lends itself to a political interpretation: the Ming emperor's celestial precincts have been breached, Jiangnan has been lost to northern armies, and loyalists have nowhere to flee.

This lyric, too, owes a considerable debt to Jiang Kui. "Drenched scents fly up to vermilion doors" reworks Jiang's well-known "The cold fragrance flies up my lines of verse."[31] Moreover, Jiang's songs to an object often contain a similar blend of imagination, aesthetic sensibility, and emotions that remains closely bound to impersonal elements within the poem rather than forming a strong, personal statement.[32]

TUNE 15, *Green Jade Table (Qingyu An)*
Recalling the Past (GZCJ, 8b)

Peach blossoms and springtime waters at Xiang River ferry.
   You cast off the boat and passed far, far away.
The setting sun's ruddy rays quivered on the distant reach.
     Flying catkins in the breeze,
     Homing geese by the clouds,
     Once and for all pointed the road to heaven's shore.

My old friend knows I'm in the sunset of my years.
   We've sung through all those backward-gazing Ba-ling lines.
The flowers fall, the wind is wild, and spring won't stay.
     These days I'm older still,
     The happy date even remoter,
     Who asked the cuckoo to make plaint?

Line 8. Ba-ling, on the bank of the Ba River outside Chang'an, was a conventional place for send-offs and departures.

In this new twist on an old subgenre, Wang reflects the intensity of his love for a friend in the clarity with which he recalls their parting. Since Chinese has no formal past tense, every detail of the original appears as if before our eyes; only after finishing the poem do we recognize the first half to be recollection.

The second stanza portrays present experience. Reaching out across miles and years, the poet clings to feelings and experiences that both can share. But the shifting spring scene before him that so resembles the first stanza's "flying catkins in the breeze" is an omen of transience. Amid forebodings that he and his friend will never meet again, a cuckoo calling "better to return" is just too cruel for the poet.

TUNE 16, *Song of the Heavenly Immortal (Tianxian Zi)*
Primal Evening (Lantern Festival; GZCJ, 27b)

Pelting down, the freezing sleet ices pearly drops.
Who decided to call *this* the "Lantern Festival"?
Back then I'd had a dream to be fulfilled tonight;
      Lonesome smoke enshrouding,
      A guttering tallow greasy.
Wintry hills cannot avail of the east wind's might.

I'd only just heard that homing swan's lament.
Now I must endure the ruined prunus' dishevelment.
Among men this day was "Primal Night's Eve";
      But men are not as before,
      And heaven hard to perceive.
Next year they'll have wiped out all Chinese calendars.

Most Lantern Day odes are a pageant of candle trees, beast-shaped lanterns, the spring's first full moon, festive throngs, and carnival treats. But for this Ming loyalist holed up in the hills Qing invasions have slain that bright dream of fullness. A drearier, chillier, more distasteful scene than stanza 1 is hard to imagine. Wang's single, feeble taper generates more smoke than light. It is too poor in quality even to weep the customarily sympathetic "tears of wax."

The poet's response to all this is grim fatalism. In the recent past, he has endured laments and disorder, and the present is only a mockery of happier years. With dry eyes and a philosopher's fortitude, he envisions a near future in which the very calendar itself will have become extinct. Of course, the new reign period and calendar adopted by the Qing could scarcely be a "Chinese calendar" for Wang Fuzhi.

TUNE 17, *Divination Song (Busuan Zi)*
Ode on a Marionette, Shown to Fellow Revelers (GZCJ, 22a)

> It does seem to bear spring woes,
> Yet whom could it ask to speak?
> Without so much as half a kindly word,
> It sticks out its lilac tongue.
>
> Red-candled shadows waver in the wind,
> Obliquely brightening a mist-wrapped moon.
> Who could discern truth in this lead-powdered lie?
> Beneath its skin, not a drop of blood.

Line 4. The lilac tongue is a conventional attribute of courtesans and entertainers.

This is at heart a simple parable about a puppet show by candlelight. Yet its progression from absence of voice to tongue, from shadows and powdered skin to absence of blood is aesthetically pleasing. The moral is pointed and gives us the uneasy feeling that Wang, too, knows how hard it can be to sift truth from lies. Scholars have argued that the prosodic rhythms in Wang's lyrics are usually closer to those of regulated verse than of the lyric, and this poem is a good example.[33] But, for foreign readers more lenient about such generic foibles, this remains a fine poem. I daresay it made a few morally spineless mandarins squirm in their seats.[34]

TUNE 18, *The Daoist Priestess (Nuguan Zi)*
A Ginger Seller's Song (GZCJ, 2b)

> I've come to sell ginger!
> Who can meet my price?
> Don't be stingy!
> As it gets old, its strands are yet denser;
> When it goes sour, its heart a deeper red.

> If it makes you slaver, don't be glum;
> If it makes your eyes tear, just wipe them.
> It's most effective in treating men's ills,
> > Be they sudden fevers or chills.

Here is Wang Fuzhi again posing, rather playfully, as folksy allegorist. Adopting a vendor's plainspoken spiel, he declaims on the virtues of cultivation. Like any cultivated Confucian gentleman, ginger remains firm in age and adversity. As the classical adage goes:

> Good herbs are bitter to the mouth, but ease one's illness;
> Loyal words grate on the ears, but improve one's conduct.

Wang's medicine, too, will make us smart a bit. The closing prescribes fortitude for men tempted by high position (Chinese regularly correlate power and prestige with heat, as in "hot official" and "cold post"). Since Wang Fuzhi's studio name was "Ginger Studio," we may well suspect that, finding like all philosophers that selling pearls of wisdom is no easy matter, Wang resorted to the hard sell.

Tune 19, *Deva-like Barbarian (Pusa Man)*
Expressing My Feelings (GZCJ, 21b)

A myriad moods cast away, my lonesome heart grows cold.
Flowers in a mirror open, fall, no image from the start.
> Just a single strand attaches me . . .
> To Middle Provinces' myriad flecks of mist.

> Dark mists cannot fly up.
> Flowers fall and follow the water's flow.
> When stones have rotted, the sea dried up.
> My lonesome heart, one fleck of loneliness.

Line 4. This recalls the conclusion to Li He's "Dream of Heaven":

> Gaze afar at the Middle Provinces: nine flecks of mist;
> A single pool of ocean waters splashing in a cup.

But, while Li He's couplet represents a mind estranged from mundane reality, Wang's represents an exile estranged from a lost kingdom.

Line 5. The language and tone of this line recall the conclusion from Su Shi's second poem on "Rain during the Cold Food Festival":

> Dead ashes cannot blow aloft.

Both poems share a mood of stoic gloom.

This poem is pervaded by a somber air of pessimistic stoicism. The first strophe creates an atmosphere of extreme chill and weariness, a sense of having seen through all comforting illusions. The poet's only remaining attachment is to the distant notion of a Chinese state. But in stanza 2, the opening's still, fatalist mood returns. The concluding oath recalls Robert Burns' "A Red, Red Rose":

> Till a' the seas gang dry, my dear,
> And the rocks melt wi' the sun.

But Burns was pledging eternal love; Wang's final vow expresses most adamantly his resolution to preserve a lonely loyalty until the end of time. We might add that, in Chinese, "lonesome" also means "orphaned," and that "lonesome" is regularly used to describe a loyal subject in exile.

Wang's style is as simple and stark as his message. It owes its effect to repeated key terms: "lonesome" occurs thrice, "heart/mood" thrice, "myriad" twice, "one" twice, "fleck" twice, falling flowers twice, and "mist" twice. Antitheses and tensions between these terms define the poem's structure and concerns: a lone, adamant heart contrasted with myriad dispositions as fleeting as fallen flowers; a single strand of uncut hair that binds Wang to his former country; and eons of time contrasted with his loyal, solitary spirit.

The worlds within Wang Fuzhi's lyrics present a clear contrast to those in the verse of Chen Zilong and Wu Weiye. Gone is any vestige of the genre's origins in boudoir and tavern. All Wang's lyrics serve to convey a literatus' "intent" and differ from his *shi* only in form. In some lyrics, Wang adopts a straightforward expression of his pain, his forebodings of mortality, and his tenacious loyalty to the vanquished Ming. Elsewhere, he conveys such sentiments indirectly, weaving self-expression into complex "odes on objects" that incorporate aesthetic and mythic elements. But patriotism is the warp thread of Wang's poetry, and Wang frequently speaks in the tone of that other high-minded exile of Chu, Qu Yuan.[35] Indeed, echoes of the *Songs of Chu* resound throughout Wang's poetic oeuvre. Wang admitted their influence when, in the preface to his *Comprehensively Annotated Songs of Chu,* he remarked of Qu Yuan: "There is a similarity in our circumstances of time and place, and our solitary spirits do resemble one another."[36] Qing critic Zhu Zumo exclaimed about Wang's lyrics: "Every word contains the spirit of the 'Lamentations of Chu'!"[37]

Language

What strikes readers of Wang Fuzhi's lyrics is that his verbal art owes so little to conventionally "lyrical" diction. The language of his lyrics is very much the language of his *shi* poetry, so it is helpful to keep the latter in mind when analyzing the former.

Wang's lyrics are pervaded by a series of images that evoke aspects of his personal experience. Images of blood, for example, recur throughout his verse. Usually, they call to mind the bloodshed of the 1640s, as in the following lyric:

> Now only vermilion maples' frosted leaves
> Fleck after fleck of blood
> Still recall those days. (GZCJ, 21a)

Other instances suggest Wang Fuzhi's sanguinary nature, as when he scoffs at a puppet whose skin conceals "not a drop of blood" (tune 17 above). In a *shi* poem from 1647, Wang wrote:

Heaven's shores, heaven's shores!
Where am I to go?
The blood in my neck, fountainlike, impatient to burst forth!
(WCSS, 531; Takata, 46)[38]

One of the commonest images in Wang's lyric poetry is the dream, which occurs at least two dozen times. Sometimes dreams retain their conventional connotations of unreality, as in:

Heaven and earth lie midst drunken dreams. (GZCJ, 21a)

Sometimes an image of dream flight expresses a fond wish, as in:

Far and remote, my dream in flight enters the layered skies;
Yet I remain, lone and afraid. (GZCJ, 10a)

Wang often invokes images of sleep and dreams to express his unshakable resolve and his patient fidelity:

Mid whale-billows and thunder-alarums my noontime dream's at peace. (GZCJ, 6b)

Obliviously I snore on, heedless of the hours;
Avici Hell seems a Fairy Isle! (GZCJ, 19a)

("Thunder-alarums" may refer to snoring. Avici is the hottest, deepest circle of the Buddhist hell.) Finally, dream imagery becomes entwined with Wang Fuzhi's hopes for "continuing the dream" of Ming rule:

Back then I'd had a dream to be fulfilled tonight. (Tune 16 above)

Mid willows and phoenix-trees,
No place to seek old dreams. (GZEJ, 26b)

Before the dream is fulfilled, don't guess wildly! (GZCJ, 6a)

At such times, Wang reminds us of Zhuge Liang as a recluse, a "Reclining Dragon" awaiting the proper time for action, as in the conclusion to "On Revisiting the Lodge for Continuing the Dream":

> A dragon in the pool snores on: all too foolish and stubborn.
> For hopes of a continuance in my waning years: too indolent!
> (GZEJ, 7a)

On the same occasion (in 1670), Wang exclaimed in a quatrain on the old "Lodge":

> My former dreams now are discontinued;
> None can match alarms from new dreams. (WCSS, 200; Takata, 223)

A large cluster of motifs serves to emphasize Wang Fuzhi's loneliness and isolation. For example, the image of a lone, failing light in gathering darkness occurs more than a dozen times in Wang's lyrics, as in the following "Odes on a Lampwick":

> Its heart still warm . . .
> Half a fleck of red, lightsome;
> A skyful of mist, darkening. (GZCJ, 5a)

> Its faint radiance tiny.
> A broken mirror's chilly rays;
> A dying firefly's last light. (GZCJ, 5a)[39]

We may compare these with a typical line from Wang's *shi* poetry:

> A drifting firefly's dying flame candles the lofty heavens. (WCSS, 215; Takata, 240)

These lines capture the excruciating sense of isolation Wang Fuzhi must have felt as a "refugee in his own country," studying and writing by lamplight in his mountain hideaway.[40] They also suggest Wang's belief that only he remained awake to the Qing's illegitimacy, that only his moral sense remained vigilant. Well might Wang Fuzhi identify with the figure of Qu Yuan, who once declared:

> All the world is muddy and I alone am clear . . .
> All other men are drunk and I alone am sober.[41]

The word *lone/lonesome* itself is perhaps the commonest in Wang's poetic vocabulary. Among more striking examples we may include:

> My lonesome heart, one fleck of loneliness. (Tune 19 above)

> Don't cast away this fleck of lonesome heart;
> Bitterly strive to hold fast its autumn looks. (GZCJ, 12a)

> Lone Peak's shadowed peak shadows a lone pine. (GZEJ, 3a)

Numerous corresponding examples from Wang's *shi* poetry include:

> Alas! sings my seventh song, my lone person lonesome. (WCSS, 533; Takata, 56)

> A lone swallow lonesome flies, espied by falcon and hawk. (WCSS, 175; Takata, 62)

Wang Fuzhi's poetry contains a wealth of images like these that engender a universe of personal symbols. We have no space to explore completely this world of migrating geese, frozen butterflies, crying cuckoos, and the like, but one more image demands our attention. Wang is fond of comparing his untonsured hair to the silken strands of a lotus plant:

> Ask the passionate, dark lotus' spun silk,
> For how much longer can it stay attached? (GZCJ, 12b)

There remains

> a single strand so fine,
> A light thread so slender,

Tethering an autumn lotus root coiling in the mud.
Let all the ruined lotus blossoms' withered leaves be done;
It will retain its numinously penetrating jadelike perfume. (GZCJ,
11b)

In the last example, Wang combines this image of a loyalist's
hair like the fibers of a lotus root with the legend of an *asura*.
According to Hindu myth, an *asura* (a kind of autochthonous
Titan) fought with Indra. After his defeat, the *asura* fled into the
hole of a lotus root. Hence, Wang's image of a wisp of hair coiling
dragonlike around the lotus root expresses his staunch unwilling-
ness to submit to Qing rule. The same conceit occurs in a number
of Wang's *shi* verses, for example,

The *asura's* single wisp coils around a muddy lotus root. (WCSS,
533; Takata, 56; compare Takata, 72, 178, 323, 343)

This image is crucial to our understanding of Wang Fuzhi; to
his dying day, Wang's hair was a potent symbol of Ming loyalism
that he risked his life to preserve. Wang's lyrics are replete with
references to hair and to gazing at his hair in the mirror, for
example:

Formerly it held the locks at my temples,
But now do they look the same?
The dark mirror consults with itself. (GZCJ, 29b)

Wang even tells us that he used to paste hairs from his comb on a
portrait of Zhong Kui, the goblin gobbler. In one quatrain, Wang
likens Chinese who adopted the Manchu tonsure to goblins and
concludes by asking Zhong Kui: "Where have you gone [now
that I need you]?" (WCSS, 96; Takata, 220).

Aside from these important symbols, we may mention a few
notable examples of Wang's skill with complex imagery. One
striking use of explicit comparison is

Frozen clouds like kohl. (GZCJ, 2a)

Among images of substitution, not very numerous in Wang's verse, we may include Goddess Mountain's "green conch mark" (tune 13 above) and this description of leaves and flowers from an "Ode on White Lotus Blossoms":

> Greenish clouds drift gently, pomade newly smoothed;
> Jade dew crisp and clear, its scent known to itself. (GZEJ, 7a)

("Greenish clouds" is conventionally used to describe the sheen of a woman's hair.) Wang employs images of transference more frequently, as in this depiction of rain:

> Heedless of the weeping willows' pearly tears aburst.
> It drips the lotus leaves to shreds, resounding for thousands of acres. (GZEJ, 6a)

Wang Fuzhi is fond of hyperbole, especially of adynaton, so common in swearing oaths and expressing resolutions:[42]

> When stones have rotted, the sea dried up. (Tune 19 above)

> When the sea is dry and the stones have rotted,
> For a thousand years it will not spoil. (GZCJ, 12a)

Although allusions are not ubiquitous in Wang Fuzhi's lyrics, as they are in his *shi* poems, they are poetically significant. Wang often reworks lines from other *shi* poets, for example:

> *Mistily* a marine sun is born from the fading night;
> *Vastly* spring on the river has gone with the old year. (GZCJ, 6b)[43]

As one might expect, Wang Fuzhi does quote from Confucian Canons in his lyrics. But references to the *Zhuangzi* are more common! Wang wrote two lyrics about Zhuangzi's philosophy; the first ends:

> Through this world of men I'll dilly and dally at will,
> Unchanging tho' the seas become mulberry groves. (GZCJ, 15b)

The first stanza of the second lyric ends:

> With a merest
> > tail-wagging through the mud,
> > Blade flashing fresh from the whetstone,
> > The entire ox cloven apart. (GZCJ, 15b)[44]

As far as lyric prosody is concerned, Wang is better known for his breaches than for his observance. One Qing critic even claimed that hardly a single lyric by Wang fits its prescribed tune pattern.[45] But, although Wang was anything but punctilious about rhyming categories and tone patterns, he did have some feel for lyrical music. Wang employs binomes frequently, his favorite being "high and far" *(biaomiao)*, which occurs at least ten times, including:

> > The Mountain Goddess has gone astray;
> > The Lord of the East is high and far. (GZCJ, 29a)

Another binome that Wang is wont to use is "drizzling mist" *(feiwei)*, which occurs at least six times, including:

> The waves' light beyond the sky, in a drizzling mist. (GZCJ, 30b)

Conclusion

Wang Fuzhi's lyrics exhibit a variety of forms and styles, so it is perilous to compare him to any one earlier lyricist. Nonetheless, a number of his adagios do bear comparison with works by Jiang Kui and his followers (see above). In particular, we sense a kinship with the lyrics of Wang Yisun (1241?–1290?), a Soong loyalist who wrote a number of long "odes on objects" that obliquely express sorrow about the fall of the Soong dynasty.[46] A few Chinese critics have noted the similarities. Wang Yisun's lyrics have been characterized as "pure-spirited" and as "sheer and lofty," and Wang Fuzhi's lyrics have been called "pure and lofty, remarkably fragrant."[47] Wang Zhong (1744–1794) observed that lyrics in which Wang Fuzhi expresses his concern about king and country by describing things rather than by directly expressing emotions recall Wang Yisun's "odes on objects."[48] The example Wang Zhong quotes from Wang Fuzhi's oeuvre is the tune *Scent of Silken Gauze*. In his preface, Wang Fuzhi writes that this lyric was written recalling a Soong philosopher who died under the delusion:

> We've recovered the northern provinces!

The lyric's first and second stanzas end like this:

> Chilly, the butterfly has forgotten the road home. . . .
> Goose-graphs, cloud-sunken,
> Find it hard to describe heartbroken lines. (GZEJ, 26b)

Wu Zeyu notes two lyrics by Wang Fuzhi that resemble Wang Yisun's work in form and style and discusses odes to the new moon by both poets that link the possibility of the fallen dynasty's renaissance with the waxing of the moon.[49] Wang Yisun's poem sighs that it will be "hard to mend the golden mirror." His figure of repairing a broken mirror finds an echo in Wang Fuzhi's lines:

> A broken mirror's chilly rays;
> A dying firefly's last light. (GZCJ, 5a)

Finally, Yan Tianyou has characterized Wang Yisun's personal style by lines from his ode "On White Lotus Blossoms":

> Its sylphen form naturally cleansed,
> Its fragrant heart even more bitter.[50]

These lines and the personal style they represent undoubtedly influenced Wang Fuzhi's lyrics.

Of course, I do not mean to overstate similarities and influences that are neither constant nor overwhelming. Wang Yisun was more the "professional" lyricist, who wielded a lyricist's prosodic wizardry and rather precious diction to create lines of great charm and cunning skill.[51] Wang Fuzhi, on the other hand, is no master of lyrical form. His odes convey their allegorical messages more forcefully and directly, and his fame does not rest exclusively on his "odes on objects." Indeed, the lyrics in which Wang adopts a more straightforward style approach the wit and imagination of Su Shi.[52]

But the links between our two Chinese loyalists named Wang are closer and are significant for our understanding of Wang Fuzhi. First, they show that Wang approved of lodging personal views in lyrics. This desire to endow a rather lightweight genre with some "substance" anticipates the position of the Changzhou school of lyric criticism. Changzhou critics were prone to declare that "words must refer to something substantial."[53] Wang Fuzhi's championing of the *Songs of Chu* and his debt to Wang Yisun's loyalist lyrics demonstrate that he, too, was partial to poetry's allegorical mode.

Second, Wang Fuzhi's imitation of Wang Yisun expresses solidarity with a Chinese loyalist who wrote against the harrowing backdrop of the Mongol invasion. In his choice of literary models, Wang Fuzhi maintained a consistently loyalist, xenophobic pose. These are the qualities that have won Wang's poetry a sympathetic audience in China among literati like Kuang Zhouyi, a late Qing adherent of the Changzhou school, who praised Wang Fuzhi's lyrics for "possessing the principle of the [*Book of*] *Odes* and *Lamentations* [*of Chu*]."[54] Wang Fuzhi's ability to infuse his lyrics with a dignified tone of moral seriousness without sacrificing aesthetic appeal represents a notable achievement. His contributions to Qing lyrics, while less appreciated, are markedly greater than those of Chen Zilong and Wu Weiye.

Chen Weisong

(1626–1682)

Chen Weisong (whom I shall call by his courtesy name "Qinian," to avoid confusion with Chen Zilong) is the first major seventeenth-century poet whose fame rests chiefly on his lyrics. Unlike Chen Zilong, Wu Weiye, and Wang Fuzhi, Qinian won little renown in other artistic genres or in the spheres of politics and thought. But he wrote 1,644 lyrics, making him the most prolific lyricist in the history of Chinese literature.

Biography

Qinian was born in 1626, the eldest son of a gentry family from Yixing, Jiangsu, just west of Suzhou's "Great Lake." His family possessed impeccable Reform party credentials; his grandfather had been dismissed in 1625 by the notorious eunuch Wei Zhongxian, and his father had helped write a denunciation that drove the odious Ruan Dacheng from Nanjing in 1638.[1] Like all the poets discussed in this volume, Qinian was precocious and well educated. Before the age of five, he began lessons with Chen Zilong! In his early teens, he studied composition with none other than Wu Weiye, who hailed Qinian as one of the "Three Phoenixes of Jiangnan."[2] Qinian passed his first-level examination in 1642 but followed his father into seclusion when the Ming dynasty collapsed. Qinian reemerged in 1655 and took a provincial level exam under Qing auspices, but he failed for the first of many times. The following year his father died. Since family finances were by now in a parlous state, Qinian set out to seek his fame and fortune.

During the next twenty years, Qinian achieved a measure of the former but hardly a morsel of the latter. He continued to seek office but failed provincial exams in 1660, 1663, and 1666. His failures do not necessarily imply any lack of literary talent on his part. The 1660s were the heyday of the Manchu nativist Oboi Regency. During Oboi's tenure, quotas for successful Chinese examinees were slashed, and many places were sold to the highest bidder.[3] The Manchu regime actively persecuted southern Chinese, so it would hardly be surprising if Qinian's pursuit of a career were halfhearted.[4] Instead, he avidly and successfully pursued pleasure.

From 1658 to 1668, Qinian rambled about the south visiting influential literati, attending banquets, and impressing potential patrons with his literary genius. During these years, he began to write lyrics and hobnobbed with such influential lyricists as Wu Weiye and Wang Shizhen.[5] The colorful and magnanimous Mao Xiang, a close friend of Qinian's father, was particularly generous.[6] Not only did Mao allow Qinian to stay in his Water-sketch Garden for ten years, but he even allowed Qinian to have an affair with a member of his entourage, the charming actor-singer Xu Ziyun.[7] With his facile brush, romantic proclivities, and full beard, "Whiskers Chen" was quite the life of the party. Yet he remained unable to provide for himself. Although influential friends managed to secure him a minor post in 1669, Qinian's profligacy left him in chronic near penury.[8]

Meanwhile, Qinian's fame as a lyricist was spreading. In 1670, he and Zhu Yizun published a volume of *Zhu's and Chen's Rustic Lyrics,* which the emperor ordered brought into the Forbidden City for his perusal.[9] In 1678, Qinian's luck finally changed. While a guest in the capital, he was recommended as a candidate for the "erudite and eminent scholars' " examination. Manchu rulers used this test to win support from disaffected Chinese gentry and to defuse criticism of Manchu rule. It provided an opportunity for dozens of southern literati who were not adamantly opposed to serving the Qing.[10] This time, Qinian was one of the lucky ones.

On passing, Qinian was named corrector in the Hanlin Academy. We might well imagine such dizzying fulfillment of his dreams would have changed Qinian, but apparently this was not the case. He continued to play the aging social butterfly with eminent friends that included lyricists Zhu Yizun and Nalan Singde. According to the conventionalized descriptions of his friends, Qinian still lived in near penury in a shabby suburb of the capital.[11] In 1682 he died at the age of fifty-six.

Qinian seemed to live his life as he wrote his lyrics, with a spontaneous overflow of powerful emotions. His revels and affairs made him a celebrity. Qinian's epitaph describes how, inspired by wine at a literati gathering, he would play the flute while songstresses crooned his latest extemporaneous lyric.[12] Several Qing literati fondly recall a painting from 1678 depicting Qinian playing a recorder, surrounded by a bevy of beauties singing a romantic lyric.[13] For Qinian to have a homosexual liaison with an actor was unremarkable, but for him to publish love lyrics written to his paramour was bold and unconventional.[14] Most accounts of his character also make Qinian seem rather naive. His epitaph records that Qinian, genial and unassuming, "never suspected the treacherous chasms underlying men's dealings."[15] Though his means were modest at best, Qinian was magnanimous and even spendthrift; he was said to "treat cash and silk like dirt."[16] As we shall see, Qinian's lyrics reflect the character of this prodigal, impractical gay blade—the incurable romantic.

Poetic Worlds

TUNE 20, *Congratulating the Bridegroom*
On an Autumn Night, Shown to Zhilu (Gong Dingzi; HHL, 26.4b)

I fling away my cap, pour out my mournful song.
Just now
    reclining by the curtain in lonesome autumn, gazing alone
        At Phoenix City's paired pylons.
An expanse of water under the Jade River Bridge,
    Undulating, glittering like snow.
Above it is the "full moon of Qin."
Long, long have I been mired in the capital;
Vexed that
    Wu salt speckles only this wayfarer's hair.
            Where is my home?
            At the end of the sky.

Leaning on high before the sights, both our hearts breaking.
My thoughts on ramparts lie with King Zhao and Yue Yi,
            Great men of their age.
White geese cross the sky, screaming like arrows,
    Screaming doom for heroes of antiquity and today.
Every last man ground down by rivers and peaks.
Tomorrow I'm off to the foot of Endless Peak;
I'll stretch that
    bowstring, slake my thirst with a brown roebuck's blood.
            In the end, what good is a
            "Rhapsody on Tall Poplars"?

Line 3. "Phoenix City" is a conventional term for the capital. The "Jade River" in the next line is Beijing's Grand Canal.

Line 6. Qinian quotes from Wang Changling's lament, "Beyond the Frontier":

> The full moon of Qin, the ramparts of Han;
> The myriad-league campaigners haven't returned.
> If only the winged general of Dragontown were here,
> He wouldn't let the Tartar horses cross the Shadowed Alps.

The "winged general" was Li Guang (d. 119 B.C.), a valorous, unorthodox, and deadly but ultimately unsuccessful commander. The "Shadowed Alps" of Inner Mongolia lie just north of the Yellow River's northern loop.

Line 12. The phrase "thoughts on ramparts" involves a pun. The phrase *guanqing* would usually mean "feelings of concern." Since the graph for "concern" also means "rampart," I have translated it that way. King Zhao of Yan and his general, Yue Yi, sought revenge for an earlier invasion by Qi. In 284 B.C., the army of Yan all but engulfed Qi. Within a generation, however, both states were overrun by Qin.

Line 17. Endless Peak lies north of Ji County, Hebei, less than one hundred kilometers east of Beijing.

Line 18. Cao Jingzong (457–508) once reminisced about his youthful hunts in the countryside:

> I rode a horse swift as a dragon, and stretched the bowstring till it sang. The arrow flew screaming, like a famished owl. In flat meadows I pursued several roebucks and shot one. I drank its blood to slake my thirst and ate its stomach to ease my hunger; it was sweet as dewy nectar. I felt a fresh wind behind my ears and fire coursing from my nostrils. Such medicine can make a man forget death.[17]

Line 20. According to legend, when Yang Xiong (53 B.C.–A.D. 18) completed his "Rhapsody on Tall Poplars," he perished of exhaustion.

Here is the sort of "powerful and unrestrained" lyric for which Qinian is famous. Its opening lines resound with his powerful subjective presence. Overt rhetoric recurs throughout the lyric, including four explicit laments, one vow, and a rhetorical question at the end of each stanza. The imagery in stanza 1 is blanketed with white, the horological color of autumn, traditionally a mournful season for Chinese poets. Sparkling snowlike water, moonlight, and hair white as salt from his homeland all intensify Qinian's melancholy.

In stanza 2, the scope of time and space expands. Qinian gazes out toward barrier passes, perhaps to Wang Changling's "ramparts of Han," where he mourns heroes who ended as glorious failures. The second strophe features the sort of graphic, violent imagery that is a hallmark of Qinian's style. Yet failures and carnage have not ground away Qinian's own heroic spirits. He concludes by anticipating the joy of the hunt, the hot spurt of freshly spilled blood.

Though it may little concern a modern audience intent on the aesthetic appreciation of Chinese poetry, we should mention that a seventeenth-century Chinese audience would surely have read topical commentary into Qinian's lyric. His skillful inclusion of the first half of Wang Changling's quatrain suggests that Qinian, too, longed for a modern "winged general" to repel the Qing's "Tartar horses." Qinian deplores Qin mastery of even China's full moon; he mourns for heroes of Yan who were eventually ground down by Qin. The poem reads sensibly if we mentally substitute "Qing" for "Qin." In this context, it is suggestive that the beginning of the last strophe can also be read:

> The Ming has sunk below the foot of Endless Peak.

On this reading, Qinian's final vow is born of frustration. Too late to fight for the Ming cause and unwilling to write rhapsodies at court, he vents his anger on a wild beast. Of course, if this were Qinian's intent, he masked it well enough to evade the Qing literary inquisitioners.

Tune 21, *Good Things Approach (Haoshi Jin)*
On a Summer Day "Shi Ju'an [probably Shi Weixi; see CJLWJ, 2.9a] invited me for a drink, so I composed using the rhymes from his poem welcoming me back from Wu for a visit" (HHL, 3.1b)

> We parted under a sky of blossoming willows:
> Snow whirling down past the sunny casement.
> Turn your head: hollyhocks embroidering their flesh;
>   Again by the railing they redly recline.
>
> Since I left, world affairs have taken a turn for the new;
>   Only we are just as before.
> When our talk turns to heroes who lost their way,
>   A sudden chilly wind soughs and blows.

Good Things Approach captures Qinian's vigorous style in miniature. The transformation of willow blossoms into falling "snow" implies the months that have elapsed since the two friends last met. The inviting hollyhocks suggest the pleasures of reunion. In stanza 2, Qinian takes stock of the recent past; nothing has changed for the better, and only his friendship has remained firm. Emotions run high as the friends broach a potentially subversive subject, and, where words reach their limit, nature amplifies with a chilling blast of wind.

The styles of stanzas 1 and 2 clash sharply, enhancing the last half's dramatic effect. Stanza 1's elegant, "poetic" diction and images of substitution yield to a bleak, prosaic response, highlighting the antithesis of tender scene and powerful feelings.

TUNE 22, *Advent of Summer (Xia Chulin)*
On the Advent of Summer "Written on 27 April 1673, using the rhymes of Yang Mengzai [Yang Ji, fl. 1365] of the Ming dynasty" (HHL, 15.7a)

> That winestruck feeling,
> Cotton-plucking season;
> Groggily, we've just seen off the spring.
> A sixth-acre pond;
> Green shadows thickly touch the curtain's folds.
> Willow flowers stirring up the sunny radiance.
> Again, on painted rafters
> jade shears fly together.
> Tea-vendors' boats are laden,
> Bamboo-shoot pickers busy,
> Mountain markets encircling.

> Suddenly, I think back:
> Thirty years ago,
> Bronze camels' griefs heaped high,
> Golden Valley's folk grew sparse.
> Scraping away bamboo powder,
> West of the railing I write up old griefs.
> Sad longings pass the time.
> Completely bored and listless,

> I finger the roses to shreds.
>   Who could know?
> Fine willows and new rushes,
> All consigned to a cuckoo's call.

Line 7. "Jade shears" is a kenning for swallows.

Line 14. When Suo Jing of the western Jin foresaw hard times ahead, he exclaimed to the bronze camels outside the palace gates of Loyang, "I'll have to see you mid thorns and briars." The famous Golden Valley garden also lay south of the western Jin capital in Loyang.

Line 19. Here, Qinian echoes Du Fu's lament for the ruined Meandering Lake Park in the Tang capital of Chang'an:

> Fine willows and new rushes, for whom are you greening?

The *Advent of Summer* contains another lament for a lost country. Qinian wields the flourishing scene in stanza 1 to throw into relief the horrors that China suffered during the mid-seventeenth century. At first, the wine-dazed poet, the burgeoning vegetation, and the bustling countryfolk all seem ripe for happiness. But such idyllic surroundings only make the poet's memories of death and destruction seem more awful. Spring's oblivious life force and fecund growth positively *oppress* Qinian, and the bustling mountain markets seem to *encircle* him. When Qinian responds by scraping away bamboo powder and by shredding roses, he seems determined to reopen old wounds, to ensure that past griefs will leave enduring scars.

The closing allusions express Qinian's mood most eloquently. Like Du Fu in "Lakeside Lament," Qinian cannot bear nature's unconcern, the cruel truth expressed near the end of "Lakeside Lament":

> We humans have feelings that soak our breasts:
> River waters, river flowers, could they ever end?

In this frame of mind, to hear in birdsong the homesick call of an exiled king is almost more than the poet can endure.

TUNE 23, *Divination Song*
Held Up by Wind at Melon Quay (near Dantu; HHL, 2.6ab)

The wind is swift, Chu skies turn autumnal;
The sun sets, Wu hills grow dusky.
Raven tallow-trees, russet pears, frost on tree after tree;
My boat stops mid the frost.

I strain my eyes at Sail-drop Pavilion;
I bend my ear for boat-urging drums.
I've heard "the endless Yangzi flows day and night";
Why not float me away?

The world within this traveler's lament hinges on the contrast between motion and stillness. This contrast informs the scene-setting first couplet, whose broad strokes and simple diction recall the manner of a High Tang couplet. The second strophe paints an autumn landscape in red, black, and white. Stanza 2 resumes the motion/rest opposition, as the poet's impatience becomes explicit. Qinian ends with a disarmingly simple plea to the Yangzi.

What distinguishes this lyric is its adroit mix of different styles. A "High Tang" couplet and an allusion to Xie Tiao's poem coexist with colloquial expressions ("I've heard" and the Wu dialect word for "me") and repetition. The word *luo* ("sets/drop") sets off "swift" and "urging"; "tree after tree" and "frost" highlight the autumn scene. "Day and night" recapitulates "sun" and "dusky," and the recurrence of "flow" as "float" energizes Qinian's homeward wish.

TUNE 24, *Pure, Peaceful Music (Qingping Yue)*
Drinking at Night in a Friend's Villa, I Hear a Youth Play the
Samisen (HHL, 3.3b)

Before the eaves, rain stops.
A spate of melancholy talk.
On the city wall, old crows are cawing.
The streetwatch drums are struck thrice.

Don't bother saving drunken ink-scriptions with silk mesh!
Just enjoy the villa's singing bells.
Why wonder at the candle flame so fiercely spluttering?
In the little tower bellows up a frosty wind.

Line 5. When Wang Bo (759–830) was a poor orphan, he stayed in a monastery where the monks despised him. But, when Wang revisited the monastery as a high official, the monks had placed protective covers of silk mesh over his temple-wall inscriptions.

Whether he was compensating for nearsightedness or just partial to night scenes, Qinian was unusually sensitive to sounds. Appropriately enough, the world within this ode on a recital is almost exclusively aural. The last drops of rain are followed by sad words, aged caws, and the strokes of midnight, all movements in a melancholy autumn sonata. Qinian then takes the stage and, eschewing all possibility of visual display, directs our attention to the music. Like the ancient Greeks, the Chinese believed that music has power to move the world by harmonizing with the macrocosmic "music of the spheres."[18] Here, notes from the *samisen* conjure up a howling wind whose frost conquers the "lampflower" (the burning wick) and whose roar shivers the candle, one last proof of the power of the acoustic over the visual.

TUNE 25, *Spring in Jiangnan (Jiangnan Chun)*
Harmonizing the Rhymes of Ni Yunlin
(Ni Zan, 1301–1374; HHL, 24.4b)

May's scenic atmosphere extends to cherries, bamboo shoots;
The fair one dallies about, the white sun is still.
The little screen's diaphanous green wafts in the east wind;
One sees nothing but the shadows of her blouse.
Without warning, a chilliness cools the spring boudoir.
At once, she recalls a piebald horse leave the village well.
"Forever these tears will darken my red kerchief;
I long to be the dust alongside my wayfarer."

He's slow to return;
Spring's hasty in departing.

Rain-threads fill the hall, and the drifting light is drenched.
The road for brocade letters so far, alas! How can they reach?
Keeping watch on hills of Wu—a whole springtime of emerald.
"What day will he win merit and return from Horsetown?
We'll both recline by the loquat tree standing tall in bloom."
In setting sunlight flying catkins turn into duckweed.
Unable to bestir them, she vainly flits about.

Line 14. Horsetown, where Han Xin was besieged by Huns in 201 B.C., lies
near Goose Gate on Shanxi's northern frontier. In the next line, "loquat"
suggests "Loquat Lane," conventional toponym for a courtesan's quarters.

When Qinian is not waxing heroic in stentorian tones, he can
play a lighter, more poignant tune. With its traditional "neglected wife" theme, its almost exclusively heptasyllabic lines, its
organization into regular four-line strophes, and its rhyme
changes after lines 6, 8, and 14, *Spring in Jiangnan* resembles an
ancient-style ballad. As it begins, the poet maintains a discreet
distance beyond the heroine's bedroom screen. Her back-and-
forth pacing seems out of harmony with the still, sunny day. As
springtime intrudes on her, stirring up restless thoughts, we move
inside the boudoir to hear her unspoken thoughts (again, as in old
ballads, it is not clear just where her "speeches" begin and leave
off). Her wish recalls that of the neglected wife in Cao Zhi's "A
'Sevens' of Woe":

> Oh, that I might become the southwest wind
> And fly far off to milord's embrace!

But in stanza 2 our heroine's wish meets a discouraging
response. With her lover so remote in distance and time, she can
only sit and wait as her springtime years slip away. Such oppres-
sion elicits another outburst, in which she comforts herself by fan-
tasizing about his return. The closing couplet recalls the rhyme
and diction of the opening lines, but time has drifted on. Day has
now become sunset, spring's catkins have fallen into a pond and
"turned into" water plants. They lie even stiller than the sunlight
in line 2, while the heroine's dallying in 1 has intensified into a

frantic effort to revive the catkins, halt the departing spring, and remain young for her absent beau.

TUNE 26, *A Halt after Crossing the Torrent (Guojian Xie)*
Before Xiande Temple, Watching the Maple Leaves (HHL, 9.5b)

> Green mists grow dense at Grass Sandal Glen.
> Circling the bank, trickling flows
> Join together covertly with Lotus and Zha streams.
> Glen sounds are mingled.
> Mid the noise of the riotous, tumbling brook,
> Something rueful, subdued, as if in response.
> The scenery here
> Wholly captures the style of Guan Tong and Ju Ran.

> Three hundred temple pines;
> Rain trickles on hoary bark,
> Frost withers kohl armor.
> Bald trunks vie in slantwise squeeze.
> In laughter we roam together;
> Yellow leaves sigh by the eaves,
> Ruddy maples wrap the temple;
> Why aren't we carrying a burial spade?

Title. Xiande Temple and the other places mentioned were located in what is now a southern suburb of modern Suzhou.

Line 7. Guan Tong and Ju Ran were renowned tenth-century landscape artists of the rugged "Northern school."

Line 15. The blithe drunkard Liu Ling was so indifferent to this world that he had his servants carry around a spade so they could bury him wherever he might happen to fall.[19]

  This lyric stands out in Qinian's oeuvre because it is primarily descriptive. Perhaps the temple and its surroundings exerted a subduing influence, for *A Halt after Crossing the Torrent* contains much less subjective rhetoric than most of Qinian's lyrics. Stanza 1 traces the downward flow of water from mist to trickle to confluent streams to riotous waterfall. The mood of stanza 2 deepens from "rueful, subdued" to ominous as Qinian describes a stand of hoary, embattled trees. All laughter pales within this copse, and dying leaves about the temple augur men's mortality.

Naturally, a poet will rarely be content to trace the course of a natural process and make a generalization about it. He will usually present a particular response to, say, the laws that waters flow downhill, aging trees topple, and all men must die. Still, the abrupt vehemence in Qinian's closure catches us off guard. It strikes a sudden blow like that of the Zen master's stick, calculated to shock us into realizing how frail and vain are human lives.

In his 1,644 lyrics, Qinian naturally explored a broad variety of poetic realms. But a trait common to nearly every one is expressive power. Occasionally, Qinian keeps his artistic distance, consigning his poetic burden to a persona like the neglected wife from *Spring in Jiangnan* or to an object like the *samisen* from *Pure, Peaceful Music*. Far more often, he speaks in his own mournful, impassioned voice, giving vent to personal woes and laments about the times. Some of Qinian's lyrics criticize inhumane policies and sympathize with commoners' suffering.[20] In most of his lyrics, however, Qinian himself is the focus of attention. His dominant mood, as Madeline Chu has pointed out, is one of "pathos."[21] Not only are Qinian's feelings usually forceful and agitated, but the scenes before him reinforce his mood with images of destruction, disorder, and desolation. Rather than submerging himself in a tranquil natural order or relegating his feelings to the inanimate subject of an "ode on an object," Qinian usually suffuses nature with the violent hues of his emotional state.

Language

Qinian's poetic diction strengthens the expressive power of his lyrics. They are dominated by vehement subjective rhetoric and by images of Sturm und Drang. The word *luan,* which has denotations ranging from "unruly" to "disordered" to "jumbled," is nearly ubiquitous in Qinian's poetry, which abounds with "unruly crows" (six occurrences), "disorderly sails" (six times), "jumbled peaks" (at least five times), and the like.[22] The words "broken" and "ruined" are barely less frequent, haunting his oeuvre with images of:

> Broken cairns and ruined stelae. (HHL, 22.6a)

> Ruined alps and remnant ramparts. (HHL, 26.3b)

The verbs typical to Qinian's poetry are equally destructive; "shatter," "crack," and "splinter" are among the commonest:

> I listen to spring birds' shattering speech. (HHL, 30.6b)

> Strumming until the icy heavens all crack. (HHL, 23.8b)

> Mountains crumble, stones splinter. (HHL, 24.11a)

Qinian is also fond of verbs like "lash" and the ubiquitous "howl" (which occurs at least forty-five times):

> Winds lash the lonely swan, waves lash the gull. (HHL, 6.7b)

> Splitting asunder with the iron dragon's drunken howls. (HHL, 3.7a)

(This describes the notes of a flute.)

> The north wind howls like an arrow. (HHL, 14.10b)

> Disorderly sails howl with rain. (HHL, 21.4a)

He ends several lyrics with the uncommon verb "sunder," for example,

> The sea-wind arises,
> The ice-cart sunders. (HHL, 11.8b)

So often the music of Qinian's imagery is punctuated by clashes and clangs. "Iron" occurs several dozen times in his verse, and the "iron flute" occurs at least fifteen times:

> Iron trunks coil and twist,
> Copper roots rise obstinately. (HHL, 22.10a)

> Up in Dragon Hall, aging iron
> Blows to splinters the hearts of waves. (HHL, 20.8a)

With such bellow and bluster, it is easy to understand why some critics find Qinian's "cacophony" grating to their ears.[23] True, Qinian can play sweeter tunes, and other critics have praised the balance between strength and grace in his diction.[24] But the dominant tone is unquestionably one of discord, or even one of ferocity:

> In setting sunlight, jumbled stelae bristle as bizarre hedgehogs;
> Atop the lofty ridge, angry boulders crouch like uncanny beasts.
> (HHL, 11.1b)

Another salient characteristic of Qinian's poetic diction is his use of colloquial and bookish expressions. Many of his lyrics feature vernacular turns of phrase, like the Wu dialect word "me" in *Divination Song* or "finger to shreds" from *The Advent of Summer* (cf. HHL, 3.2b). At the other extreme, Qinian wrote a number of lyrics employing the sententious rhythms of classical Chinese prose (for examples, see HHL, 25.10b, 30.9b). Qinian's daring expansion of the lyric's vocabulary betrays the influence of Xin Qiji, well-known for experimenting with popular and bookish language five hundred years previously.[25]

Qinian is the first lyricist we have encountered whose typical syntactic constructions deserve careful scrutiny. Since self-expression is the dominant theme in his poetry, the propositional language Qinian uses to convey a lyrical response helps define his personal style. Qinian's lyrics have been called the "culmination of the powerful and unrestrained school," so it is not surprising that his poems abound with forceful subjective rhetoric.[26] Characteristically, Qinian's responses are direct, emotional reactions rather than complex thoughts or subtly modulated moods. His commonest expressions include "Why wonder?" (with eight occurrences), as in:

> Why wonder at the candle flame so fiercely spluttering? (tune 24 above)

"How to foresee?" (eight times), as in:

> How to foresee that phoenix would leave and simurgh be orphaned; (HHL, 19.2b)

"I mistook" (eight times), as in:

> I mistook it for a sketch of the distant mountains' brows; (HHL, 13.8b)

"mournful amazement" (three times), as in:

> Affairs old and new,
> Evoke mournful amazement; (HHL, 12.10b)

and "vexes [or "rues" or "saddens"] to death" (six times), as in:

> At heaven's border, vexing me to death,
> One wheel of the full moon . . . (HHL, 30.2a)

In his less pessimistic moments, Qinian is wont to speak of "manly fellowship" or "unrestrained spirits" (these and similar phrases recur at least twenty times in his lyrics), as in:

> Manly fellowship, powerful and unrestrained. (HHL, 17.7a)

Elsewhere, Qinian spends a great deal of time talking of heroes, valor, and swordsmanship. This is typical behavior for sons of

Ming loyalists, who were much taken with knight-errantry and derring-do.[27] More often, Qinian turns melancholy when "talk turns to heroes who lost their way" (tune 21 above) or when he wonders:

> Where are the heroes now? (HHL, 21.3a)

But the most frequent trope in Qinian's arsenal of responses is recollection. So often does Qinian indulge in nostalgia that I counted at least twenty-five poems that begin with a memory. I gave up counting lyrics whose second stanza begins with "recall . . ." at seventy-five. Indeed, if I could choose only two words to suggest the tenor of Qinian's oeuvre, they would be "recalling disorder."

We might expect Qinian's poetic closures to end with a bang, a final explosion of violent scenes and stentorian cries. To be sure, some of his conclusions positively bristle with passion, for example:

> The candle flame reddens,
> My whiskers are like pikes! (HHL, 12.10a)

Yet, considering Qinian's ponderous style, many of his closings are remarkably light. Often, he concludes by turning from grief to a source of consolation or pleasure.[28] Elsewhere, Qinian ends with a bitter, sardonic laugh, much in the manner of Xin Qiji.[29] A large number of lyrics end with a mood of weary bleakness, for example:

> Chill and forlorn, old dreams all betrayed. (HHL, 20.5b)

> On a swathe of empty river
> Echo sounds of sparse rain. (HHL, 21.8a)

Since Qinian's poems often begin like a lion and charge onward like a rhinoceros (in fact, Zhu Yizun and others marveled that Qinian possessed the spirit of a "black bull," referring to an epi-

thet originally describing Xin Qiji's heroism), it is fascinating to
see so many stagger to a close, drained of all life and movement.[30]
Many even end with a plaintive reference to speech, suggesting
the poet's inability to converse or evoking the mournful tones of
creatures given voice by the pathetic fallacy:

> Of my heart's affairs, with whom could I speak? (HHL, 5.7a)

> > With the swallows
> > I speak of my life. (HHL, 6.9a)

> A crying cicada bemoans its pain, speaking in my place. (HHL,
> 26.2a)

> Now
> the woeful one's zither-borne tears drop like lead.
> Note after note forms the rainy casement's idle words. (HHL,
> 30.1b)

(The "tears" are sad music, and the words could be spoken either
by people near a rainy casement or by rain outside the window.)
These examples demonstrate that Qinian's patterns of lyrical
response are subtler and less monotonous than previous critical
opinions and superficial readings might suggest. While Qinian
can howl and bang with the best of them, he can also end with a
murmur or a whimper.

Like most Qing lyricists, Qinian makes abundant use of allusions. Like nearly all lyricists, Qinian makes most of his references to earlier poetry. Among these, references to Du Fu's poetry
are common enough (for an example, see tune 22 above). Qinian
is fond of Bai Juyi's "Lute Song," which he quotes or paraphrases
half a dozen times, for example:

> For manly fellowship, who'd insist on old acquaintances? (HHL,
> 19.1b)

which recalls the famous couplet from Bai's "Lute Song":

We have both washed up on heaven's shore;
For a chance meeting, who'd insist on old acquaintances?

As is customary for lyricists, Qinian alludes frequently to Late Tang poetry. He seems to have felt a special attraction for the weird, extravagant imagery of Li He. For example, Qinian refers to "leaden tears" a dozen times, including:

> Bronze immortal in the moonlight,
> Tears falling like lead. (HHL, 19.10a)

This alludes to Li He's "Song of the Bronze Immortal Leaving the Han":

> Recalling his lord, he shed pure tears like molten lead.[31]

Qinian is also wont to borrow from Soong lyricists. Among his more striking allusions is the "sour wind":

> A gust of sour wind rolls up angry billows. (HHL, 5.4b)

This is derived from a famous line by Wu Wenying:

> On Arrow Creek a sour wind impales the eyes.[32]

The most common Soong source for Qinian's literary allusions is the verse of Su Shi. Qinian adapts Su's well-known line:

> Startling billows slap the bank[33]

and intensifies the waves' violence by substituting "angry" for "startling," for example:

> At Northern Fastness, clamorously, angry billows howl. (HHL, 8.1a)

Nor are Qinian's borrowings from Su Shi limited to Su's lyrics. Qinian is especially taken by Su's conceit that traces of our past are like

> . . . a flying swan that trod on snowy mud.
> Happening to leave in the mud a talon mark. . . . [34]

Among Qinian's eight references to this poem, we may cite the conclusion to the following lyric:

> A swan flying with snowy talon:
> Bygone affairs hard to detain. (HHL, 18.9a)

Of course, Qinian also borrowed many gentler, more sensuous lines from lyric poets. The preponderance of his allusions, however, serve like most of his verbal artistry to create a "powerful and unrestrained" mood.

Like Su Shi and Wang Fuzhi, Qinian is a literati lyricist rather than a musician lyricist. His use of rhyme categories betrays a southerner's accent, while even "the number and tones of syllables are often at variance [with accepted tune patterns]."[35] Of course, such irregularities do not prove that Qinian was insensitive to musical prosody, only that he refused to be shackled by it. In fact, his lyrics are liberally spiced with reduplicative, alliterative, and rhyming binomes. Oddly, one of the most common (with more than fifty occurrences) is *linglong* ("cute and delicate"), which expresses a less common aspect of his style. Truer to the dominant tone of Qinian's lyrics are a flock of binomes expressing personal griefs. *Chouchang* ("sadly longing") is the commonest (more than fifty occurrences); *qiaocui* ("haggard and worn"), *cuotuo* ("slips and stumbles"), and *lingping* ("lone stumbling") all contribute to the moods within his lyrics, for example:

Sadly longing, I recall my past life. (HHL, 5.4b)

Alas, for a myriad problems' slips and stumbles. (HHL, 17.8a)

Qinian is also wont to cloud the waters with binomes like *menglong* (fifteen times) and *hongteng* (fifteen times), both of which mean "blurred and hazy." A related word is *yixi* (faint and indistinct), whose nearly fifty occurrences usually involve fading memories, for example:

> Bygone affairs, faint and indistinct. (HHL, 9.9a)

A last major category of binomes are onomatopoeic ones. Qinian's favorites, no surprise considering the gusty flavor of his lyrics, are *sasa* (twelve times) and *souliu* (5 times), both of which describe the mournful sighing of wind. All these binomes serve to prove the obvious point that Qinian had an ear for verbal music. After all, the fellow was accomplished enough to accompany performances of his lyrics on the recorder. As we mentioned, music, especially flute music, forms a significant recurrent motif in his oeuvre. Of course, we should not forget that the flute in Qinian's lyrics is likely to be blasting forth iron howls.

Conclusion

Qinian's erudite, multifaceted lyric oeuvre naturally recalls much earlier poetry. Lyrics used to be called "music archive ballads" *(yuefu)* to indicate their filiation with an earlier popular genre performed to musical accompaniment. Qinian's literati lyrics recall the literati imitation ballads written by Cao Zhi and other Jian'an poets. Their starkly realistic, or even naturalistic, depictions of political chaos at the end of the Han dynasty find a distinct echo in Qinian's work. Cao Zhi's poetry, with its turbulent, restless quality and forceful, dynamic spirit, particularly brings Qinian to mind. Similarly, the mix of social criticism and forthright delivery in many of Qinian's lyrics recalls the "new music archive ballads" of Bai Juyi. In fact, Qinian has been credited with "applying the spirit and expressive techniques of Bai's ballads to the lyric."[36] We should not underestimate the impact and significance of verses like Qinian's "The Boat-tracker's Lament"[37] or of lines like these recalling Chinese in 1645 who were:

> Indentured within the house walls,
> Press-ganged atop the city walls. (HHL, 2.7b)

But unquestionably Qinian's closest affinities lie with the literati lyrics of Su Shi and Xin Qiji. For example, He Guangzhong has noted the resemblance between Qinian's *Divination Song* and Su's lyrics.[38] Su Shi also wrote a famous *Divination Song* in which he expresses the melancholy thoughts of a literatus lodged in a temporary riverside dwelling. Moreover, there is something of Su's style in the way Qinian weaves a poetic world from simple, repeated words. He Guangzhong also observes that several lyrics that Qinian wrote to the tune *Congratulating the Bridegroom* resemble Xin Qiji's lyrics.[39] The *Congratulating the Bridegroom* that I translated above shares the mournful, martial air of lyrics like Xin's "Parting from Cousin Maojia."[40] Both are forceful, complex meditations on history and personal fate written in a powerful, "masculine" style.

Although Qinian manages to capture the heroic expansiveness that forms one facet of Su and Xin's lyric achievement, this is only a partial victory. One measure of Su and Xin's greatness is their ability to explore a variety of poetic worlds in a wide range of styles. As James Liu has written, "Su Shi has often been called the founder of the 'powerful and free' school of the lyric, but this description does scant justice to the scope and variety of his lyrics."[41] Irving Lo has admired "the remarkably wide range of [Xin's] style: from earthy humor and colloquialism to high reaches of philosophical speculation and the fecundity of his learning, from moods of the deepest melancholy and tenderness to the most spirited outbursts of high-minded sentiments."[42] Qinian could match neither the wit nor the profundity of these illustrious predecessors. Consider such typically complex meditations on time, history, and personal fate as Su's "Recalling Antiquity at Red Cliff" or Xin's "Cherishing Antiquity at Northern Fastness

Pass in Jingkou."[43] While Su waxes "powerful and unrestrained" in describing

> Random rocks pierce the air,
> Startling billows slap the banks,

he can still turn and laugh at himself

> . . . for being so sentimental
> And growing grey hair so soon!

While contrasting his own lot with a glorious past of

> Gold-tipped spears and ironclad steeds,
> Tigerish esprit bolting a myriad leagues,

Xin is still able to conclude with a self-deprecating comparison with a famous aging general, asking,

> Can he still bolt his rice?

That witty second "bolt" helps bring out the ironic contrast between then and now. But Qinian, whose lyrics are rarely as sublime or as visionary as Su's or Xin's, nevertheless gets caught up in his heroic persona. He never shows the ironic detachment that would enable him to rise above his performance and look down with a transcendent laugh. I imagine that this is what Yoshikawa Kojiro intended when he remarked of Qinian's lyrics, "A hero can fool people."[44]

To be sure, Qinian did attempt to make lyrics more respectable by enlarging their scope and elevating their moral concerns.[45] But I cannot agree with Madeline Chu's thesis that Qinian achieved any unprecedented elevation and expansion of the lyric.[46] In fact, Qinian failed to attain either the subtlety or the breadth of his Soong models. On the other hand, Zheng Qian's criticism that Qinian was "coarse and reckless, cacophonous, a devil or yaksha among lyricists" is surely too harsh.[47] It is best to recognize the affective power of Qinian's best poetic worlds and the skill of his verbal art while conceding his limitations and the uneven quality that is inevitable when an artist tries to produce more than sixteen hundred inspired works. Hence, I conclude that Qinian is a major lyricist of the seventeenth century; Qinian is not, however, the finest of the early Qing lyricists.[48] His lyrics should be ranked a notch lower than those of Wang Fuzhi.

Zhu Yizun

(1629–1709)

Zhu Yizun enjoys considerable fame as a scholar and poet. Zhu has been called an "ultra-erudite."[1] His learned writings include a *History of the Hanlin Academy,* an anecdotal history of Beijing and its environs entitled *Old Tales under the Sun,* and the monumental *Investigations into the Meaning of the Canons,* a 297-chapter bibliography of scholarship about the Chinese classics.

Zhu also won acclaim as poet and anthologist. His one hundred–chapter *Compilation of Ming Poetry* and its commentary has been quite influential.[2] His twenty-six–chapter *Compilation of Lyrics,* though hampered by the scarcity of Soong texts and by Zhu's own partisan views on the lyric, has been widely read. Its selections and introductory remarks formed the foundation for the "West Zhejiang" school of lyrics founded by Zhu.[3] Zhu's *shi* poetry has been paired with that of Wang Shizhen as the finest written during the early Qing, and Zhu's collected works also include 518 lyrics selected and edited by the author.[4]

Biography

The fount of all this scholarly and literary activity was born on 7 October 1629 in the village of Sparkling Waters, part of Jiaxing, Zhejiang. Zhu Yizun was the eldest son of an illustrious literati family who had been in decline for two generations. Zhu was notably precocious, and no doubt his parents hoped he would embark on an official career and restore their fortune. Unfortunately, the collapse of the Ming put an end to this possibility. In 1640–1642, as Zhejiang suffered from severe famine and uprisings that Magistrate Chen Zilong was struggling to ease, the Zhu family often had to go without food.[5] They remained so poor that in 1645 Zhu was humbly *married into* a more solvent local gentry family. Sparkling Waters was a hotbed of anti-Qing resistance, so Zhu Yizun and his family spent the next four years moving from place to place, dodging bandits and marauding Qing troops in an effort to find a haven.[6] By 1650, Zhu was finally able to settle down and earn his living and reputation as a teacher.[7]

In 1656, Zhu ventured to Guangzhou, where he served as tutor to the magistrate's son. For the next twenty years, Zhu interspersed travel with stints of service as secretary to officials in Zhejiang (1660–1663), Shanxi (1664–1667), Shandong (1668–1670), Hebei (1673–1677), and Nanjing (1677–1678). In one lyric, Zhu sighed of this period:

> I try counting on my fingers:
> In the past twenty years,
> How many days spent in my garden at home? (PSTC, 1.38a)

Zhu made good use, however, of the chance to gather an impressive collection of stone rubbings and calligraphic specimens and to rebuild his library. The Zhu family had burned its books in 1662 to avoid prosecution during the "Ming History Case," in which they had unwittingly become entangled when Zhu Yizun bought a copy of Zhuang Tinglong's ill-starred history.[8]

We may note in passing that Zhu maintained extensive relations with Ming loyalists. He attended the 1650 meeting in which Wu Weiye attempted to revive the Ming "Restoration Society."[9] Zhu admired the poet and Ming loyalist rebel Qu Dajun; when they met in Guangdong, Zhu even wrote the preface for a volume of Qu's verse and extolled Qu's noble intent.[10] Zhu also befriended Ming loyalist thinker Gu Yanwu and helped defend him when he was accused of sedition in 1668.[11] Aside from a few suggestive passages in Zhu's lyrics, however, there is no evidence that Zhu himself was an active Ming loyalist.

Rather than leading him into trouble, Zhu's far-ranging travels and extensive network of influential friends won him some fortune and fame. By 1669, the proceeds from his career as secretary enabled Zhu to buy a small estate in Sparkling Waters, which Zhu named "Bamboo Knoll" (Zhu's own sobriquet became "Bamboo Knoll").[12] In 1678, Zhu was recommended to take the "erudite and eminent scholars' " examination.

Passing this exam meant glorious and almost overnight success for Zhu. He became a corrector in the Hanlin Academy, assigned to help with the officially sponsored Ming History Project. During the next four years, Zhu enjoyed a dizzying succession of imperial favors. Zhu was thrice chosen as a top-level examiner. In 1681, he became an imperial tutor, responsible for the emperor's Confucian education and for fielding the "Kangxi emperor's" incessant, probing inquiries.[13] In 1683, Zhu was selected to serve in the Imperial Library, to live within the Forbidden Palace, and to receive a steady stream of gifts from the Imperial Kitchens.[14]

Unfortunately, Zhu's meteoric rise to favor had also won him a few enemies. As one of four commoners who had passed the 1679 exam, Zhu was despised by "career members" of the Hanlin Academy. In 1684, they seized a pretext to impeach him, remove him from office, and expel him from the Forbidden City.[15] In 1689, Zhu was restored to office for a brief period, but in 1692 he returned south for good. Zhu's chronobiography claims that Zhu's family remained poor, but in 1696 Zhu did build his "Pavilion for Sunning Books," from which derives the title of his collected works.[16] In his last years, Zhu remained surprisingly spry, traveling widely in the south and continuing to write prose and verse. He was granted audience with the Kangxi emperor on three of the ruler's southern visits; in 1705, the emperor bestowed on him an honorific tablet proclaiming Zhu "Scholar of Classics and Erudite of Affairs."[17] Zhu died at the age of eighty on 14 November 1709, the only one of our seventeenth-century poets to survive into the eighteenth.

None of Zhu's biographers provides us with much sense of Zhu Yizun's character. He appears to have been a man of some passion. Zhu is supposed to have had a romance with his sister-in-law; after her death, he wrote a long and remarkably candid account of his love for her.[18] Despite the pleas of his friends, Zhu insisted on retaining the poem in his collected works. He retorted that he would willingly suffer posthumous shame and even forfeit his share of ancestral offerings:

> I'd rather not partake of two pantries full of ham,
> Than excise "Romantic Feelings' " two hundred rhymes![19]

Although some have questioned this anecdote, Zhang Shaozheng observes that Zhu's romantic lyrics, published on the death of his sister-in-law, are entitled *A Taste for the Zither in the Dwelling of Modest Intents*. "Modest Intents" was the sister-in-law's courtesy name.[20] In addition, Zhu dedicated at least a dozen poems from his *Collection from the Rivers and Lakes, Laden with Wine* to songstresses (one is, in fact, addressed to a singer—see PSTC, 3.30a). One of these lyrics is addressed to a songstress nicknamed White Cur, with whom Zhu allegedly had an affair.[21] Zhu was widely attacked for such "lewd" lyrics by men who felt that lyrics should express only edifying and uplifting sentiments, but Zhu's decision to retain them in his collected works conforms with the expressive component in his view of literature.[22] Zhu argued that great literature must express strongly felt, sincere emotions with daring:

> The adage has it that "though the heart should be great, the gall should be small." Only in poetry is this not so![23]

But the passion that dominated Zhu Yizun's life was rather a scholar's love for ancient culture. If we can believe his chronobiography, Zhu was precocious in heeding Tao Qian's exhortation:

> Measure your might, hold to that ancient track;
> Though surely you'll be cold and famished.

As a hungry thirteen-year-old, Zhu astounded his relatives by declaring:

> With robbers and rebels north of the Yellow River, and cliques and factions within the Imperial Court, upheaval is fast approaching! What's the use of pursuing current arts [i.e., examination essays]? Better to discard them and study antiquity![24]

To this mistress Zhu was faithful all his life. The burning of his family library must have been a tragic blow to Zhu, and he spent the next forty years acquiring a library that, by 1700, held over eighty thousand volumes.[25]

Zhu's passion for books is best illustrated by two anecdotes about him, the "Beautiful Swindle" and the "Beautiful Impeachment." The former occurred when a collector refused to give Zhu a peek at some rare manuscripts. Zhu then threw a party for all the local literati, which the collector attended. Zhu lavishly bribed the collector's amanuensis, borrowed the volumes overnight, and engaged an army of copyists to reproduce their contents.[26] Zhu's enemies secured a pretext to impeach him in 1684 when Zhu was caught smuggling an unauthorized person into the Hanlin Academy. The intruder was a copyist whom Zhu had engaged to reproduce rare official documents for Zhu's history of the institution.[27]

Unsurprisingly, book learning is a central plank in Zhu's literary esthetics. He once admonished a grandson:

> All students of verse and prose must base themselves on the Canons and Histories before they can deeply penetrate the ancients' innermost apartments.[28]

The key term in Zhu's writings on poetry is "orthodox elegance" (*ya*).[29] Indeed, the West Zhejiang school of lyrics associated with Zhu soon became identified with imitation of the southern Soong masters of form and with excessive use of allusive ornamentation.[30] Most critics absolve Zhu himself from charges of narrow partisanship and slavish imitation, but nearly everyone agrees that the great bibliophile's concept of poetry suffered from terminal pedantry.[31]

Poetic Worlds

TUNE 27, *Riverful of Red*
Tomb of the First Emperor of Wu (PSTC, 1.8a)

> Marble benches, moss-clad;

I bow

> to his likeness, red-whiskered as of yore.

Imagine those days:

> Master Zhou and Young Lu,
> Their fame rang through the age.
> Begging for food: how could he heed Zhang Zhao?
> Lifting his cup: he toasted only Gan Ning.

Watch:

> midst small talk and laughter he fends off Cao and Liu
> And partitions China.

> He divided north and south,
> Straddled the Yangzi River.
> His watchtowers arose,
> His white flags rused.

Sigh for

> The Six Dynasties' divided rule;
> Afterward, who could succeed him?
> His branch-temple still stands on this site of dragons and tigers;
> Spring and autumn men never cease offering up boars and fowl.

What's left:

> hills encircle withered grass, the parapets are empty;
> The chilly tide beats on.

Title. The emperor was Sun Quan (r. 222–251).

Line 3. Among Sun Quan's greatest generals were Zhou Yu (175–210) and Lu Xun (183–245).

Lines 5–6. Zhang Zhao (156–236) was a cautious courtier who advocated appeasing the northern forces of Cao Cao. After his victory over Cao at Redcliff, Sun Quan rebuked Zhang, saying, "Had I followed your plan, we would now be begging for food!" Gan Ning (fl. 212) was a hawkish general who ridiculed Zhang Zhao's policies. During his toast before the victory at Redcliff, Sun urged Gan to put national security above factional disputes.

Line 7. Cao Cao's son Cao Pi (r. 220–226) founded the Wei dynasty in the north; Liu Bei (r. 221–222) founded the Shu dynasty in Sichuan.

Line 12. At the battle of Redcliff, the Wu navy managed to approach and burn most of Cao Cao's fleet by disguising an incendiary vessel with white flags of surrender.

Line 15. The original ancestral temple of the Wu dynasts stood near modern Suzhou. When Sun Quan moved the capital northwest to strategic Nanjing (the "site of dragons and tigers"), he built a "branch-temple" there.

Riverful of Red creates a pessimistic world in which past glories are irrevocably buried, never to be revived. In the course of stanza 1, we witness the speaker at Sun Quan's tumbledown temple fusing his perspective with history, communing with Sun Quan and his age. "Bow" conveys the speaker's respect for Sun, "Imagine" depicts the past taking shape in the speaker's mind, and "Watch" marks the climax of his identification with the Three Kingdoms' period.

In stanza 2, the vision recedes. The first strophe echoes stanza 1 with a succinct list of Sun's exploits. The lead-in word "sigh" punctuates the speaker's regret that Sun Quan had no worthy successor. Though Sun's traces can still be sought at historical sites and in popular cults, his heroic legacy remains intestate. Like Wu Weiye (see above), Zhu also concludes with multiple references to Liu Yuxi's "Recalling the Past at Nanjing"; "What's left," "withered," "empty," and "chilly" effectively convey Zhu's *ubi sunt* theme. Where only hills "encircle" and only the tide "strikes," no southerner will be able to emulate Sun Quan's martial vigor.

TUNE 28, *Flower-selling Song (Maihua Sheng)*
Petal-raining Terrace (PSTC, 1.9ab)

> Withered willows at Whitegate Bay.
> The tide returns from lashing the city wall.
> Little Longbluff adjoins Big Longbluff.
> Song-clappers and wine-pennants, all scattered and lost;
> Only fishing-poles remain.

> Under autumn grasses, the Six Dynasties turn cold.
> Petals rain on the empty altar.
> Where no one else remains, I lean a while by the railing.
> Swallows in the setting sunlight come and go;
> Such rivers and mountains!

Line 1. Whitegate was the western gate of Nanjing and, by synecdoche, another name for the city.

Line 3. During the Six Dynasties, Longbluff was one of the liveliest parts of Nanjing.

Line 6. Poets commonly imagine the Six Dynasties to be buried under autumn grasses. See, e.g., Du Mu's line "Six Dynasties' culture and artifacts: grass extending to the sky."[32]

Line 9. Almost inevitably, Zhu alludes to Liu Yuxi's "Raven Robe Lane":

> By the side of Vermilion Bird Bridge wild weeds blossom;
> At the mouth of Raven Robe Lane evening light slants.
> Swallows who once dwelt in the halls of Wang and Xie
> Now fly into the homes of ordinary folk.

Petal-raining Terrace, which was mentioned in Wang Fuzhi's *Groping for Fish,* was rebuilt on a height a few leagues south of the Qing city of Nanjing. It afforded an extensive view of the city, the surrounding hills, and the Yangzi. For Zhu, as for most Chinese poets, a vista in space provides the inspiration to "cherish the past."[33] Stanza 1 describes the site's present desolation, in contrast to Nanjing's sixth-century heyday. One cluster of images associated with the Yangzi evokes constancy; the bay, tide, bluffs, and fisherfolk have presumably changed little over the centuries. But the beleaguered city wall, songstresses' clappers, and wineshop pennants have proved mutable.

The first strophe in stanza 2 again juxtaposes elements of the past that have departed with those that remain. The Six Dynasties are interred even in memory, but a shower of petals briefly brings them back to life. Zhu's meditation on the vicissitudes of historical time continues with his allusion to "Raven Robe Lane" swallows, which evokes both loss and permanence. But the conclusion encompasses a wider vista that has endured all human vicissitudes. Note the impersonal tenor of Zhu's lyric. As the poet concentrates on interweaving cosmic and historical perspectives, his individual response remains implicit.

TUNE 29, *Butterflies Lingering over Flowers*
Revisiting Tsin Temple, Inscribed on a Wall (PSTC, 1.29a)

Through ten leagues of drifting vapor, hills approach, recede.
　　　As soon as the light drizzle ceases,
　　　　I'm delighted that springtime sands have softened.
Again the fragrant grasses fill the horizon.
Year after year by the River Fen I watched the homing geese.

Tethering my mount to a green pine: it's still before my eyes.
　　　I come again to this scenic spot,
　　　　Dimly recalling that youth's splendors have changed.
Profusely as before, the chilly moonlight brims.
Shining on me as I climb alone the streambank by the bridge.

Title. The Tsin Temple stood along the Fen River, near modern Taiyuan, Shanxi.

In this lyric, on the other hand, Zhu Yizun relegates the historical and cosmic perspectives to the background. The ancient temple and changing season provide mute commentary to Zhu's meditation on change and continuity in his own life's course. Stanza 1 recounts his passage to the temple; its second strophe reveals that Zhu has spent many years traveling away from home. Strophe 2 also suggests the ancient temple's desolate condition by echoing a Niu Jiao couplet:

> Don't you see, now on the River Fen,
> Year after year, only autumn geese fly.

In stanza 2, memories of his youth flood back. The tethered horse, youthful splendors, and chilly moonlight suggest a former tryst or nighttime revel. Now only the aging poet prepares to cross the bridge.

The salient artistic feature of *Butterflies Lingering over Flowers* is its extensive use of aspect. The images and actions in nearly every line are held in a particular light or attitude, whether "as soon as," "again . . . fill," "still before," or "as before." These phrases constitute what traditional critics would call the "veins and arteries" of the lyric; they control the circulation, distribution, and pulse of time within the poem. As befits a riverside meditation, time in this ode flows to a Heraclitean beat. Even the hills seem to shift, and waxing spring only emphasizes the waning of old age. Memories and moonlight argue for the past's persistence, but the poet's recall is dim, and the moonlight may be mere reflections in a river whose flow is the central symbol of change and passage.

TUNE 30, Long Halt Lament: Adagio
On Geese (PSTC, 6.6a)

They've befriended how many mournful autumn comrades?
Purposefully, year after year,
The north wind sweeps them past.
Purple Fortress' gate is lonesome,
Golden River's moon is cold;
Who could vent their sorrows?
Curving cays and winding holms.
Yet they only long to live in Jiangnan.
They alight at will on the level sands,
Cleverly arranged as staggered *koto* frets.

At Parting Reach.
They're wont to fly off startled, without rest;
Most likely skittish of ruined lotuses and light showers.
One string at the cloud-tips,
Look:
graph after graph of suspended needles, drooping dewdrops.
Gradually
they slant askew and weakly flutter down;
Just as

our eyes send them off to a sunset sky of indigo gauze.
    Unable to write of longings,
Once again
    they fly off, sprinkled on chilly waves.

Line 4. Purple Fortress is also called "Goose Gate." The Golden River flows through Inner Mongolia, near Guisui, Suiyuan.

Line 15. Celebrated calligrapher Mi Fu (1051–1107) compared his brushstrokes to needles and dewdrops.

This is Zhu's most famous "ode on an object," one whose mournfully expressive tone has won enthusiastic praise from traditional critics.[34] The descriptions in stanza 1 are laced with melancholy adjectives and verbs. During their arduous, lengthy journey in the first three strophes, the geese are poignantly expressive. The fourth strophe cleverly combines an image of weary geese at rest with musical expressions. "Geese alight on level sands" is not only the title of a well-known Soong painting of the Xiao and Xiang region, but it is also the title of a song for stringed instrument. It slyly foreshadows the "koto" in the next line.

The beginning of stanza 2 recapitulates stanza 1's first three strophes, reattributing various woeful sentiments to the geese. The last three strophes continue the virtuosic wordplay from stanza 1's conclusion. Playing on the conceit that geese in formation resemble "goose graphs," Zhu also manages to convey the pathos of these long-range travelers.

This lyric is marked by witty paradoxes. The narrator is as reluctant as the speakers in many late southern Soong poems characterized by a "retreat toward the object," yet the lyric's "impersonal" emotions are quite moving. Zhu's speaker resembles Flaubert's ideal narrator, who is "everywhere present but nowhere apparent."[35] The narrator asserts that geese are incapable of expressing sadness; they are but a stringless "koto," incoherent scribblings. Yet from beginning to end the geese enable Zhu to express—with ink—his sadness. In this sense, they have indeed "written of longings."

TUNE 31, *The Spring Breeze Undulates (Chunfeng Niaonuo)*
On Roving Willow-threads (PSTC, 5.2b)

Ask

> Lord of the East to apply his might
> And tether tight spring's glories.
>> They thread the little path,
>> And splash the sunlit sand.

Just now

> gloomy clouds encage the sun,
> Hard to find "wild horses";
> A light squall stains the grass,
> Binding up autumn serpents.
> Swallows kick them up, again they descend;
> Orioles bear them away, off they glide;

Stirring all the yellow whiskers of countless blossoms.
Even if they were allowed to waft over the vermilion doors,
Still they'd fret for men's shadows beyond the window-mesh.

> Mournful longings by Mlle. Xie's pondside pavilion;
>> Xiang curtains suddenly rolled up;
>>> As she stares outward
>> They approach and brush the rafters.
>>> The sparse fence binds,
>>> The short wall screens.
>> A faint breeze through the villa,
>> Fine scenery in someone's estate.
>> When red sleeves beckon,
>> They insist on following the gauzy fan;
>> Where a jade whip drops,
>> Again they pursue the scented carriage.
>> Don't disdain them for fickleness,

Laugh

> that they're affectionate, like me;
> Spring hearts unsettled,
> Dreaming in flight at heaven's shore.

Line 1. The "Lord of the East" is the morning sun.

Lines 6–8. "Wild horses" is an old image of substitution for drifting vapors.[36] The "autumn serpents" are conventionally used to describe sinuous calligraphic forms.

This ode on an object is considerably lighter in tone. Its shiftless, airy manner admirably suits the character of its subject. From the opening whimsical demand to the final fanciful comparison, poet and catkins are afflicted by springtime restlessness. The second strophe features alternate-line parallelism marked by lively substitutions of "wild horses" and "autumn serpents" for the catkins. As we follow the drifting floss, it traces a voyeuristic route past homes of the wealthy, a courtesan's pavilion, and a lover's carriage. Like the catkins in Su Shi's famous *Water Dragon Chant* that "have thoughts, insentient as [they] may be," these "willow-threads" are constantly being tangled up in human emotions.[37] But Zhu's lyric is breezier and carries less freight of sorrow. No less than thirty-seven of its 124 graphs are verbs, most of them active verbs that create images of transference. This lavish use of personifying verbs enhances the lyric's ornate, yet dynamic style.

TUNE 32, *Divination Song* (PSTC, 4.2ab)

A fading dream encircles hills on the screen;
"Seal graphs" melt in a mist of fragrance.
All day a swathe of window drapes hangs low;
The swallows speak, but people don't.

Grass in the courtyard now enveloped in mist;
Willows by the gate ready to drift catkins.
Having listened to all the pear blossoms in last night's wind,
Tonight there's rain at yellow dusk.

Lines 1–2. A manifold screen either decorated with mountain landscapes or folded like peaks and valleys was a common boudoir appurtenance. So were cakes of incense carved with archaic "small seal" graphs.

This *Divination Song* is a fine example of the "oblique and concise" style that most traditional critics held to be the sine qua non of Chinese poetry. Though Zhu's speaker is again "nowhere apparent," every detail of the late spring evening reflects his or her mood. "Fading," "melt," "hang low," and "mute" create an atmosphere of loneliness and imminent loss. In stanza 2, the speaker's gaze moves outside the curtains, but the melancholy mood is, if anything, intensified by misty grass, drifting catkins, sunset rain, and the last rustlings of fallen pear blossoms. The pun on "pear" and "depart," both pronounced *li* in Chinese, emphasizes that spring is passing away rapidly.

Divination Song is a triumph of "implicit rhetoric"; in the manner of a Wen Tingyun lyric, it expresses a mood without psychological exploration or explanation about *whose* feelings are being conveyed.[38] It fulfills a central desideratum of traditional Chinese aesthetics:

> Without setting down a single word,
> Fully capture the wind's free flow.[39]

TUNE 33, *Silk-pounding Song (Daolian Zi;* PSTC, 4.2a)

> Mist swirls lithe,
> Rain drizzles on.
> Beyond blossoms, an east wind chills the cuckoo.
> Climbing alone the little tower, no one else sees
> The heartbreaking spring sights return this year.

This lyric, while a bit less "oblique," is even more concise than the last. It presents a wistful, delicate world of misting rain, chilly breezes, and a little tower overlooking the springtime. The speaker watches alone and sorrowing, though sorrow is ultimately displaced to the scene itself. What makes this *Silk-pounding Song* outstanding (in Chinese) is its smooth rhythmic flow. Lines 1 and 2 feature reduplicative binomes, and the last four lines all rhyme. Actually, since the tune pattern prescribes no rhyme for line 4, and since it ends with an oblique tone rather than with a level tone, line 4 is only a "near rhyme." But it does help impel the lyric to a strong close that also leaves a lingering taste of words left unspoken.

TUNE 34, *Water Dragon's Chant (Shuilong Yin)*
Paying Respects to Zhang Zifang's Tomb (PSTC, 3.2ab)

Back then at Bolang, a leaden awl—
Alas—it missed the Qin Emperor!
    An enormous search in Xianyang,
    He fled for his life to Xiapei;
    Staying in one piece wasn't easy.
    Even when the Han arose,
    Had Harn still existed,
    Would he have served Liu Bang?
Reckon:
    To appraise his merits with the three heroes'
    And be enfeoffed with Liu's myriad households;
    None of this was his lifetime ambition.

His relic of a temple in Pengcheng's old village.
There's grayish moss, broken stelae across the ground.
    1000 coils of the post-route;
    Alps abrim with maple leaves;
    One inlet of the river waters.
    The man from Blue Sea has gone back;
    The stone of Yi Bridge lies hidden;
    These ancient walls vainly enclose.
Longingly,
    with forlorn white hairs,
    Wiping tears as I pass,
    I face the setting sun.

Title. Zhang Liang (d. 189 B.C.) helped Liu Bang found the Han dynasty in 206 B.C. and was done in for his troubles not long after.

Line 2. Zhang was a scion of the old state of Harn, which was obliterated by the first emperor of Qin. Zhang once tried to assassinate the emperor at Bolang (modern Yuanyang, Henan). After the attempt failed, Zhang managed to evade a massive manhunt and flee southeast to Xiapei (modern Pei County, Jiangsu), the hometown of Liu Bang.

Line 10. The "three heroes," Liu Bang's righthand men, were Xiao He, Han Xin, and Zhang Liang. Zhang was enfeoffed as marquis of Liu, in modern Pei County, Jiangsu.

Lines 17–18. Zhang once studied rites with the mysterious "Gentleman from Blue Sea"; he provided Zhang with a strongman who helped in the attempt on the Qin emperor's life. Zhang later received esoteric books of strategy from a wise man who called himself "Lord Yellowstone" and who claimed to be a rock under the Yi Bridge.

In this lyric "cherishing the past," Zhu adopts a more personal approach to relations with history. Stanza 1 is an act of imaginative sympathy, recapturing the moral crises in which Zhang Liang proved his heroic mettle. Zhu shows great sensitivity to this fighter against tyranny; in line 2, both poet and subject seem to share that "Alas!" On reading strophe 2, we realize that Zhang fled only to fight again. Strophe 3 emphasizes Zhang's enduring loyalty to his old country; joining forces with Liu Bang was just a means to settle an old score with Qin, and winning fame or merit was not Zhang's motive for action.

Stanza 2 turns from the historical to the individual perspective. Zhang's legacy now lies in ruins, but not forgotten. The poet's own tortuous journey to the temple contrasts with Zhang's desperate flight in stanza 1. The time for such heroics has passed, and the magic from Zhang's age has disappeared. Zhu concludes with a heartfelt response; an old man burdened with sad recollections, he faces the sunset that signals an ebb both in personal vigor and in political fortunes. It may be reading in too much to see pro-Ming sentiments in *Water Dragon's Chant.* But, given the emphases on resistance to Qin tyranny and on the importance of loyalty to one's old country, I imagine a Qing official would have found Zhu's lyric uncomfortable reading.

Zhu Yizun's lyric oeuvre may be divided into poems that explore events and sites from his years of travel (the 210 lyrics in his *Collection from Rivers and Lakes, Laden with Wine*), poems on objects (the 114 lyrics from his *Tea-steam Collection Depicting Objects*), and poems that delineate longings from the boudoir and garden (the eighty-five lyrics from *A Taste for the Zither in the Dwelling of Modest Intents*).

The first collection contains songs that recall old loves and banquets, that send off or miss old friends, and that record visits to historic sites. The songs are almost always written in the first person, expressing the sentiments and sensibility of an itinerant literatus. Unlike the verse of Chen Weisong (Qinian), however, Zhu's songs do not present us with a forceful poetic persona. Quite often, Zhu's depiction of his present mood and circumstances pales before the past. It is the intensity and vividness in Zhu's relationship with bygone men and events that distinguish many of his travel poems. In one typical lyric to the tune *Song of 100 Syllables,* Zhu paints in the first stanza a desolate frontier landscape at the rugged Juyong Pass and begins stanza 2 by exclaiming:

> Who unleashed ten myriad Yellow Turbans
> —The ball of mud left unsealed—
> To race right through Cart-chassis Pass? (PSTC, 1.18b)

(The Yellow Turbans were rebels who nearly brought down the Eastern Han in A.D. 184; during the Han interregnum, rebel Wei Xiao's general requested, "Please give me but a ball of mud, with which I will seal up Hangu Pass!") These allusions provide the dramatic climax to a lyric that ends by quoting another exasperated slight to a usurpatious general:

> Dong Long really was a chicken, a cur!

Zhu Yizun's odes on objects, like most examples of the genre, are attacked by critics who esteem the personal emotions visible in poetry. In the odes on objects by Zhu and others, emotions are usually ascribed to insentient things, while the speaker's own feelings rarely appear close to the surface (for exceptions in Zhu's odes, see the conclusions to *Long Halt Lament* and *The Spring Breeze Undulates,* tunes 30 and 31 above). Most of Zhu's odes on objects are vehicles for displaying his skillful description, imagination, and wit. Zhu tends to invest his subjects with just enough "feeling" to make them poignant without projecting his feelings too awkwardly or heavily. Many critics complain that Zhu produced "glutted" lyrics whose gross surfeit of sensuous imagery is uninformed by higher sentiments.[40] But it is only charitable to point out that a poem need not convey the *author's* feelings to produce a satisfying aesthetic effect, as long as it achieves the desired effect on its audience. In his best odes on objects, Zhu Yizun is able to do just that.

The songs from *A Taste for the Zither in the Dwelling of Modest Intents* present familiar worlds that hearken back to lyrics from the Five Dynasties. Against a setting of ornate boudoirs and enclosed gardens, a succession of (usually) female speakers sigh over their lost loves, absent paramours, and groundless ennui. Most are written in an "oblique and concise" manner, though a few (such as *Groping for Fish,* PSTJ, 4.8a) embody complex and enigmatic mixtures of memory and desire, and a few are frank and straightforward. Consider the second stanza of *Song of the Southern Tower;* after having enumerated a world of passing spring sights, the speaker exclaims:

> Lament that homeward dreams cannot come true.
> Feelings at departure are even dearer.
> Regret:
> at heaven's shore, no way to deliver scented notes.
> Wishing to speak of an affair from this day, last year,
> But how many like last year's person can remain? (PSTC, 4.13a)

Zhu's lyrics in this vein are widely considered to be his best, not because they explore new worlds, but because they dress up familiar ones so elegantly.[41] Critics wax enthusiastic about Zhu's refined style, which is usually characterized as "profoundly elegant and deeply appropriate."[42] Yoshikawa Kojiro extols Zhu's ability to "use florid, exalted diction to express refined and implicit thoughts."[43] These traits distinguish most of Zhu's lyric oeuvre and color most of his poetic worlds, for Zhu Yizun is very much a poet of "dulce and decorum."

Language

Zhu Yizun's verbal art strikes the same note of refined elegance. Zhu does occasionally leaven his lyrics with colloquial language, as in:

> Ah'm about all in! (3.29a)

(Zhu is using the Wu dialect word for "I".) But, despite his extensive use of allusion, Zhu almost never reproduces in lyrics the prosodic rhythms and function words found in Chinese classical prose.

The images in Zhu Yizun's lyrics are mostly those deemed appropriate by hallowed generic convention. Zhu's odes are stuffed with the "piebald horses," "inlaid [or "fragrant"] carts," "painted eyebrows," fancy stationery, "magic rhinoceros-horn," tiny slippers, and "gauzy stockings" that decorate the erotic landscape of so many lyrics.

I don't necessarily agree with Jiao Xun, who argued that lyrics were appropriate for expressing only the softer, "feminine" side of one's character, whereas prose should be reserved for expressing "male" character, but Jiao's comment does hold true for Zhu's lyric diction.[44] Zhu uses the words "soft," "weak," and "tender" at least forty times in his lyrics. He refers to "tender oars" at least six times, while "soft words," "tender souls," "pliant twigs," and "tender bowels" all recur:

> Pliant waves, unbroken. (PSTC, 4.3b)

> I ask her tender soul, did you ever make this flight? (PSTC, 4.6a)

> Her soft words entreating. (PSTC, 4.22b)

> Her tender bowels dissevered. (PSTC, 4.19b)

("Severed bowels" are the Chinese equivalent for our "broken heart.") Zhu is fond of such delicate, even precious imagery. His favorite color word is "alcedine/emerald," while his favorite adjective appears to be "fine/delicate." "Delicate waists," "delicate hands," "delicate paces," and the like occur with numbing frequency. Even Zhu's favorite lead-in words, "afraid" and "longingly," evoke the "feminine" yearnings that Zhu so often expresses within his lyrics.

It is no surprise, then, to discover that the texture of Zhu Yizun's poetry is dominated by textile imagery. Terms for cloth, weaving, silk, and shearing are to be found in nearly every ode. Even when the topic has nothing to do with textiles, Zhu often employs substitution or transference to create a sense of long, clinging strands:

> Closeknit rain trails its strands so fine. (PSTC, 4.16b)

> One strand of the Autumn River. (PSTC, 4.11b)

A prime source of conflict in Zhu's verse is the contrast between a prevailing finespun, lingering, yearning (since "silk" and "longing" are homophonous in Chinese) atmosphere and images of "severing" or "shearing." The word "shear" occurs more than thirty times in Zhu's oeuvre, for example:

> A sour wind shears and shores. (PSTC, 2.30b)

> Behind my back, she shears a strand of fragrant cloud. (PSTC, 4.16a)

> Her spring blouse sheared close, her light veil flimsy. (PSTC, 4.2a)

("Fragrant cloud" refers to a woman's billowy locks.) The word "sever," a common one in Chinese poetry, recurs with uncountable frequency in Zhu's oeuvre. Among a plethora of images such as "broken stelae," "severed bowels," "sundered souls," and the like, the following examples stand out:

> The ruined stele lies broken, I can't decipher its fish and crawlers. (PSTC, 1.24a)

(Zhu has used images of substitution for the sinuously cursive forms of old inscriptions.)

> I cannot find the severed bridge. (PSTC, 3.4a)
>
> Who understands her sundered soul. (PSTC, 4.23a)

(A "sundered soul" is one that has taken flight to find a lover and then lost its way.)

The moments of greatest tension within Zhu's lyrics occur when their tender, delicate fabric collides with sharp, injurious figures, for example:

> It blows asunder a single string of young wild geese. (PSTC, 3.14a)
>
> Her tender bowels dissevered. (PSTC, 4.19b)
>
> Completely unafraid of the beauty's gauze fan,
> Their delicate wings vibrate:
> One shear of lock-clouds in disarray. (PSTC, 6.23b)

(Zhu is describing dragonflies in flight, whose beating wings resemble a woman's "cloudlike" disheveled locks.)

> She longs for a strand of red silk to tether him tight. (PSTC, 6.15a)

("Him" refers to a swallow, who at the end of the lyric is described as "one pair of Bingzhou shears." Since swallow-tails are "shearlike" by convention, the heroine's efforts to keep the swallow faithfully near her side are doomed to failure.) In this context, it is small wonder that the compound "faltering" (literally "sever-continue," *duanxu;* note the presence of the "silk" element in "continue") occurs several times in Zhu's lyrics:

> Unable to keep him;
> Her parting song falters. (PSTC, 2.23a)

> Sure to recall my faltering dream. (PSTC, 3.12, conclusion)

As we might expect from a poet so fond of the clever, circumlocutory wordplay required for writing odes on objects, Zhu Yizun has a tendency to use complex imagery. Similes are not so common, though we may cite:

> The wind arouses fallen flowers like sleet. (PSTC 1.30a)

> Grassy scars, as if shorn. (PSTC 6.18a)

Images of substitution are numerous and, in Zhu's songs on objects, nearly ubiquitous. Most are quite conventional; among the fresher, more striking substitutions are

> Green phoenix-trees trail their teats. (PSTC, 1.1a)

(Phoenix-tree pods are called "teats"—cf. PSTC, 6.7b.)

> Horse-teats trail from the vines. (PSTC, 1.39a)

("Horse-teats" are a kind of wild grape. Zhu was apparently fond of mammary images, for he wrote an ode on breasts—see PSTC, 5.14b.)

> In the lamp still sways a single fleck of "red-bean." (PSTC, 4.24a)

(Zhu substitutes for the candle's flame a tree associated with longing, the "red-bean" being another name for the "missing you tree.")

I see:

> spring pennants now unfurling;
> Green spears still untried. (PSTC, 5.3b)

(Each line contains an image of substitution for tealeaf sprouts.) Rarely does Zhu pass up the opportunity to enliven his lyrics with a bit of transference, for example:

> The broken stele dozes on the square plinth. (PSTC, 1.18a)

> Their shadows interweave on the bank of sunny sedge. (PSTC, 6.23b)

("They" are dragonflies.)

Zhu Yizun's closures exhibit a considerable range of effects. It is most notable, however, how often he ends on a sad, subdued note. Conclusions like the following example are numerous:

> Twilight bells on the ancient bank;
> Fishermen's lights chill beyond the casement. (PSTC, 3.6a)

Zhu closes with a reference to speech no less often than does Chen Weisong, but the voices in Zhu's work are much gentler and more timid:

> Soft words in the sounds of flying insects. (PSTC, 4.9a)

> Together we listen to bean blossoms whisper. (PSTC, 3.4b)

> Shadows on the screen speak softly. (PSTC, 5.7a)

Endings like these may have contributed to some critics' impressions that Zhu's lyrics are "hollow" and "devoid of forceful qualities of spirit."[45] Yet occasionally we do find a conclusion with a bit more verve, such as this quite colloquial closing:

> Even if Chengdu dyed a dozen kinds of stationery,
> They couldn't write down all the bitterness of yearning. (PSTC, 1.15b)

On the whole, however, Zhu's adherence to "oblique and concise" aesthetics prevented him from writing many forceful, assert-
ive endings.

A salient characteristic of Zhu Yizun's verbal art is his masterful manipulation of allusions. Most of his references are to earlier
poetry, especially to anecdotes and images with sensual appeal.
Zhu regularly alludes to "a maiden's face mid peach blossoms"
(e.g., PSTC, 3.3a, 1.2b), to the woman who "peeped over the
eastern fence at Soong [Yu]" (PSTC, 1.9b, 1.13a), to "washing
skirts" (PSTC, 2.12a, 4.3b; cf. tune 38 below), and the like. Sometimes Zhu refers to bolder tales, as when he calls his time spent in
the north a stay "in the marketplace of Yan," where knights-
errant like Jing Ke and Gao Jianli used to drink (see PSTC, 2.14a,
2.26b). But usually Zhu's references are to more elegant poets like
Li Shangyin and Jiang Kui:

> Left behind merely to accompany the sad one,
> Listening through eternal night to rain on the brushwood gate.
> (PSTC, 5.23a)[46]
>> At this moment, little boys
>> Trap them in spiderwebs by the eaves. (PSTC, 6.22a)[47]

Zhu Yizun has a special knack for matching allusions within a
parallel couplet. Among his more striking juxtapositions are

> There remains
>> The barren mound after a white cock dream;
>> The setting sun by Vermilion Bird Bridge. (PSTC, 2.7a)[48]
>
>> The beast-brocade shuttle is tossed;
>> The mermaid-pearl tears are finished. (PSTC, 4.18a)

(The former image is a weave with animal motifs; according to
legend, mermaids wept pearls that could be woven into cloth.)

> I see:
>> burning reeds against a swan sky;
>> The ebbing tide at Fish Quay. (PSTC, 6.25a)

(For our purposes, it is enough to appreciate the mood of lofty wildness and rustic pleasures without further exegesis.) Zhu is equally adept at weaving allusions into "line-skipping couplets." Aside from the example above (tune 31), we may add:

> Lord Mountain's emerald
> Heaps about the county gate.
> Fragrant Bay's whiteness
> Flows by the tree roots. (PSTC, 3.17a)

(Zhu describes sites near Jiangyin, Jiangsu, with historical associations that it would be tedious and irrelevant to explain here.)

One more aspect of Zhu's allusive skill is his fondness for "collecting lines" from earlier poets and adapting them into new poems (Zhu adapted 109 such lyrics in his *Exotic Brocade Collection*). This practice is often dismissed as merest "pastiche," lacking even a shred of creativity.[49] Most readers would laugh if I claimed to write great verse by lifting lines from *Bartlett's Quotations* or if I placed independent artistic value on such verse, like Paul Valery in Borges' short story attempting to *recreate Don Quixote,* word for word. Yet so successful are lyrics like the following that I wonder if the sum of Zhu's adaptations does not sometimes far exceed the value of its parts.

TUNE, *Song of the Heavenly Immortal*
Grudging Spring['s Departure] (PSTC, 7.26a)

Where to meet you along the green willow road?
A myriad springtime voices arise at Southern Reach.
Indigo clouds, fragrant grasses nestle, side by side;
> Don't you complain!
> That parting's bitter.
Even more, when the green spring's sun has nearly set.

Last night the easterly wind entered my door again.
The swallows haven't come back, flowers bear the rain.
This morning who was it that wrenched out the blossoms?

Spring has gone.

Not to be detained.

To this place I come alone, vainly circling the trees.

Line 2. Southern Reach is a conventional place of departure (cf. tune 14 above).

If you pretend to be unaware that Zhu borrowed every line from a different Tang poet, you will probably agree that this poem breathes with a unique life of its own and stands independently of its sources. Wang Shizhen was so impressed by Zhu's adaptations that he exclaimed, "This is demonically skilled!"[50]

One last trait of Zhu's lyrics is their meticulously proper prosody. Many critics have asserted that, among early Qing lyricists, only Zhu Yizun obeyed punctiliously the Soong rhymes and tone patterns.[51] Of course, his flawless prosody does not mean that Zhu was necessarily more sensitive to the music of lyrics than his less painstaking peers. One Qing critic sighed that, "when prosodic manuals for lyrics arose, the study of lyrics was crippled!"[52] We can, however, still discern musical qualities in Zhu's verse. He employs binomes often; unsurprisingly, the most common is "dainty and delicate" *(xianxian),* which occurs a dozen times, for example:

> Dainty and delicate, with tiny steps she goes to the window. (PSTC, 4.20b)

But, whether or not Zhu Yizun was especially sensitive to the musical aspects of lyric composition, his attention to prosody is significant. It betokens a key trait of Zhu's oeuvre, his allegiance to the formal beauty of southern Soong lyricism.

Conclusion

The wide range of Zhu Yizun's lyrics suggests an equally wide range of poetic models. Zhu's broadminded attitude about uses of the poetic tradition is revealed in his comment:

Short tunes ought to be modeled on those from [before the fall of the northern Soong capital at] Bianjing. Adagio lyrics should imitate those from after the Southern Crossing [i.e., the southern Soong].[53]

As we have seen, Zhu's shorter "boudoir lyrics" and expressions of idle sentiments closely resemble those by the *Among the Flowers* poets and those by northern Soong upholders of the "oblique and concise." Some of Zhu's longer, more impassioned works, on the other hand, recall the "literati lyrics" of Su Shi or even of Chen Weisong (for an example, see tune 20 above). But the bulk of Zhu's lyric oeuvre takes its model rather from southern Soong formalist poets. In his critical writings, Zhu stressed this filiation, as in the influential preface to his *Compilation of Lyrics:*

> When men of this age speak of lyrics they invariably praise the northern Soong, but only in the southern Soong did lyricists perfect their skill.[54]

Zhu's rediscovery of the southern Soong masters marked a turning point in the development of seventeenth-century lyrics, and his own lyrics frequently praise southern Soong lyricists like Jiang Kui, Shi Dazu, and Zhang Yan:

> I love best Jiang and Shi. (PSTC, 2.16a)
>
> I reckon that Yaozhang is the finest of the lot. (PSTC, 1.4b)

(Yaozhang is Jiang Kui's courtesy name.)

> For filling in new tunes, I feel closest to Jade Field. (PSTC, 2.25a)

("Jade Field" is Zhang Yan's sobriquet.) The lyrics of Jiang, Shi, and Zhang share a family resemblance; all are elegant, imagistic, meticulously crafted, and often quite impersonal. It is easy to find lyrics by Zhu Yizun that recall verses by any of these three figures. The similarity to Jiang Kui is least striking, for Jiang's lyrics are generally distinguished by a certain "harsh and gaunt" quality that we rarely find in Zhu's work.[55]

The links between Zhu Yizun and Zhang Yan are cited most often, and Zhang's influence on Zhu is indubitable. Zhu's *Long Halt Lament* (tune 30 above), in the manner of Zhang's best-known lyrics, conveys a genteel melancholy in a "pure and spare" style.[56] The resemblance is enhanced when we recall that Zhang's ode on a migrant goose was so famous that he became known as "Lone-goose Zhang."[57] But Zhu's adagios are not often so mournful; the sense of aesthetic distance is greater than that in Zhang's lyrics. Chen Tingzhuo, who admired Zhang Yan's laments for the southern Soong, commented that Zhu Yizun lacks Zhang's "profound melancholy."[58] Yoshikawa Kojiro, seeing the obverse side of the stylistic coin, praises Zhu for lacking Zhang's "chilly and sour" manner.[59] Qing critic Wu Hengzhao correctly points out the considerable stylistic gulf between Zhang and Zhu: "While Jade Field's lyrics are sparse, Bamboo Knoll's are meticulous and formal; while Jade Field's lyrics are bland, Bamboo Knoll's are refined and exquisite."[60]

Though few enough critics have mentioned them, I find considerable resemblances between the lyrics of Zhu Yizun and Shi Dazu. Both excel at odes on objects that have been characterized as "pure and fresh," "suitably smooth, lightsome and full."[61] Zhu's *Spring Wind Undulates* is a perfect example of this style.[62] Of Shi's songs to objects, we may cite some representative lines from *Pair upon Pair of Swallows:*

> Then they softly speak,
> Conferring to no decision.
> Wafting swiftly they fly, brushing flower-tips;
> Alcedine tails parting pink shadows.[63]

Readers of Zhu's lyrics will find "soft words," "alcedine," and shearing swallow tails all quite familiar. Moreover, Zhu's affinity to Shi Dazu extends beyond their songs on objects. For example, Qing critic Ding Shaoyi has pointed out that the following lyric by Zhu Yizun is indebted to a similar lyric by Shi:[64]

TUNE, *Autumn in the Cassia Palace*[65] (*Guidian Qiu;* PSTC, 1.6a)

> Thinking of a vanished affair,
> I cross the riverside bluff.
> Green mothbrows lowly glitter as Viet hills look back.
> Together we napped in a boat, listening to autumn rain . . .
> A little mat, a light quilt, each separately chill.

TUNE, *Swallows Return to the Roofbeam (Yan Guiliang)*[66]

> Lying alone by an autumn casement, cassias still not fragrant.
> Afraid that raindrops will waft along the chill.
> The jade one appears alongside Chu clouds.
> She, too, bears tears
> Throughout yellow dusk.
>
> A west wind tonight, the phoenix-trees are cold.
> Decidedly, no dreams
> Of bridal ducks.
> Twenty-five notes of autumn gongs resound.
> Asking each to endure
> Our separate thoughts.

These melancholy autumn reveries evoke a common atmosphere and share so many words that further comparison is superfluous.

Of course, I do not wish to claim that Shi Dazu lurks behind every lyric that Zhu Yizun wrote. I freely admit that the stylistic distinctions made between the lyrics of Jiang Kui, Shi Dazu, and Zhang Yan are subtle and vulnerable to counterexamples. The general resemblance between their lyrics and those by Zhu Yizun, however, is unmistakable. We might also ask why Zhu chose southern Soong adagios for his poetic model. After all, many southern Soong lyrics bemoan the loss of northern territories to Ruzhen invaders who were ancestors of the Manchus. Zhang Yan, for example, was a Soong loyalist who obliquely lamented his country's fall to the Mongols in elegant, meticulous odes on objects. Like Wang Fuzhi, Zhu Yizun advocated elevating the lyric through the use of allegory:

> Though the lyric is a minor art . . . one can borrow the bedroom
> words of lads and lasses and infuse them with the significance of the
> *Li Sao* and the deviant *Capitol Odes*. [67]

Zhu Yizun's advocacy and emulation of southern Soong loyalist
poetry very likely had a special significance to Ming loyalists.

Zhu Yizun was once considered preeminent among early Qing
lyricists. Only later, when the Changzhou school of lyrics sup-
planted Zhu's West Zhejiang school, did his reputation suffer.
Changzhou critics and their heirs have attacked Zhu precisely for
a lack of allegorically expressed feelings, for a deficiency in "true
and compelling thoughts."[68] Many critics also complain that
excessive fondness for allusion makes Zhu's lyrics obscure and
weakens his ability to express an individual sensibility.[69] Zhu can
be defended on grounds that his lyrics surely were not obscure to
a lettered seventeenth-century audience, while his constant involvement with the literary past lies at the very core of Zhu's individual sensibility.

Still, the criticisms contain a moiety of truth. Zhu's lyrics, like
those of Shi Dazu, are rather lightweight; we suspect his facility
with words outstrips his ability to conceive of elevated, sublime
poetic realms. Unlike poets of the "heroic and unrestrained" sort,
Zhu was too decorous to create a forceful, compelling lyric persona. Instead, Zhu mastered all styles of the lyric, displaying
genius at none. Nevertheless, Zhu Yizun is a major lyricist of the
seventeenth century. Zhu's revival of the southern Soong style,
his versatility, and his cunning verbal art constitute the most significant contributions to the early Qing lyric we have seen so far.

Nalan Singde

(1655–1685)

A common reaction to the story of Nalan Singde is one of incredulity. Here was a young Manchu who learned mounted archery as a child, who served his emperor in the Imperial Bodyguard, and who died at the age of thirty. How could he possibly have imbibed enough of the Chinese literary tradition to have mastered completely one of its most demanding verse forms, the lyric? Yet Singde's lyrics are the most popular and widely annotated of any Qing poet; Wang Guowei hailed Singde as the finest lyricist since the northern Soong.[1]

Singde's was an age when Han Chinese resented their alien conquerors and when Manchu conquerors mistrusted Chinese literati. How could the son of a Manchu grand secretary possibly gain the friendship and admiration of the realm's greatest scholars? Yet Singde's lyric anthology was edited and printed by noted poet Gu Zhenguan (see below); Singde befriended, hosted, and exchanged poems with men like Zhu Yizun and Chen Weisong. After Singde's death, his collected works in twenty chapters were published by renowned scholar Xu Qianxue (1631–1694), who had served as Singde's tutor, examiner, and mentor. How are we to explain this Manchu phenomenon, whose dramatically precocious appearance and tragically premature departure so astounded seventeenth-century Chinese literati?

Biography

Singde was born in 1655 to Mingju, a prominent Manchu prince, and his wife, a granddaughter of the Qing's "Grand Progenitor," Nurhachi (r. 1616–1626). Singde grew up within the Forbidden City. Apart from a few excursions as a bodyguard with the imperial entourage, he lived his entire life in Beijing. Mingju, whose tastes ran to Chinese art and antiques, engaged famous literati to instruct his sons. Singde exhibited the precocity customary of Chinese poets, but with a Manchu twist.[2] To complement his photographic memory and facile brush, Singde was also credited with proficiency in mounted marksmanship.[3]

As his father rose to power through office in the imperial household, Singde studied diligently. Aided by liberal quotas for Manchu civil service candidates and by the benevolent supervision of Examiner Xu Qianxue, Singde passed his provincial examination in 1672. Ominously, Singde was too ill to attend the "presented scholar" exam held the following spring. It was during this time that Singde married a Ms. Lu, daughter of a Chinese bannerman official, and began to pursue his literary avocations of scholarship and patronage.[4] Singde started to compile his "Miscellaneous Jottings from Clearwater Pavilion," a collection of trenchant observations on his studies.[5] Clearwater Pavilion, tucked away in his father's estate in a northern suburb of Beijing, was Singde's haven. To the literary banquets he held there came nearly every important Chinese scholar of the time, excluding those who were unwilling to serve in Beijing.[6] At about this time, Singde produced his first volume of lyrics, the "Cocked Hat Collection," and his fame as a poet began to grow.[7]

In 1676, Singde passed his "presented scholar" exam and, as a member of the prestigious Plain Yellow Banner, was selected to be an imperial bodyguard. In this capacity, Singde accompanied the Kangxi emperor on many imperial expeditions, traveling to the Ming tombs (1676), on hunting trips (1677, 1679), on summer retreats (1678, 1680, 1681), on a tour to Manchuria to worship imperial ancestors (1682), and to Jiangnan (1684). In late fall 1682, Singde accompanied a state mission north to the Amur River region to investigate Russian incursions.[8] Meanwhile, Singde's literary prowess outshone even his career. In 1678, Gu Zhenguan published Singde's "Drinking Water Lyrics"; the title suggests not only a temperance uncommon among young noblemen but also Buddhist piety. It alludes to a Zen metaphor for enlightenment: "When a fish drinks water, he himself knows if it is warm or cold."[9] In 1676, Singde joined a campaign to rescue from Manchuria one Wu Zhaoqian, a Chinese literatus persecuted during the 1657 Examination Scandal. Thanks partly to the influence of Mingju, Singde and his friends managed to secure Wu's return by 1681. Ever since, Chinese have fondly remembered Singde for his role in the rescue.[10] There is no telling how much more Singde might have accomplished in literature and politics. Unfortunately, when the emperor embarked on his customary summer excursion in June 1685, Singde was on his deathbed. On 1 July he died.

Singde impressed contemporaries with his unassuming character. One observer wrote of the young Manchu:

> His natural endowments are incomparably flourishing, yet he is meek as the humblest commoner. He amuses himself by playing the zither and singing, by appraising calligraphy and paintings, seemingly unaware that he is the son of the grand vizier.[11]

Singde appeared remarkably indifferent to fortune, fame, and high rank. According to one authority, Singde "much preferred a life of scholarly retirement to the formality and decorum of court or the rough-and-tumble world of national politics."[12] Of course, we must be cautious about inferring Singde's attitudes from his writings, for expressing indifference to fame and high rank is often de rigeur in literary composition. When Singde was consoling a friend whose career hopes were gloomy, for example, it was only fitting to express soothing sentiments like:

Since antiquity, hard for a lofty talent to be eminent (YSCJ, 480; a
lyric addressed to Gu Zhenguan; cf. tune 37 below)[13]

Actually, Singde pursued his own career sedulously and with
great success. As one biographer has noted, Singde appears to
have been a most circumspect and discreet courtier.[14]

Why, then, was he so miserable? This is the question that has
beguiled and bemused all students of Singde's life and works.
None has raised the specter of the intentional fallacy, the possibility that the wretchedness pervading Singde's lyrics may be due to
generic convention, not to lived experience. I, too, tend to dismiss
the possibility, for Singde espoused the traditional Chinese notion
that "poetry expresses intent," and the tone of his *shi* poetry is
just as lugubrious as that of his lyrics.[15] It is irresistible to read
Singde's lyrics as a faithful record of at least one important aspect
of his character.

Some scholars point to the loss of his wife in 1677 as a cause of
Singde's melancholy. Certainly the death of so young and cultivated a bride must have devastated Singde, as his numerous elegies to her attest (e.g., YSCJ, 124, 274, 278, 290, 325, 354, 473, 495,
504). But Singde wrote of misery before 1677, too, and other scholars cite the constraints of palace life and noble station on Singde's
soul. His friend Yan Shengsun once wrote that Singde lived his
life "fretting with worries, like one approaching [a deep torrent]
or treading [on thin ice]."[16] To be sure, life in the household of
China's most powerful official involved more than its share of
intrigues, struggles, and insecurity. Singde saw a number of his
friends banished, demoted, or enmeshed in factional politics.
Though we do not know how Singde viewed his father, Mingju is
now seen as a greedy, unscrupulous power broker.[17] Only three
years after Singde's death, his father fell from power; among
Mingju's impeachers was his erstwhile ally (and Singde's mentor)
Xu Qianxue.[18]

Whatever his reasons, Singde's view of life was a grim one. The
peculiar blend of passion and pessimism in his poetry suggests a
young man suffering from acute Weltschmertz, as in the following
cry from the heart:

TUNE, *Recalling a Beauty of Qin (Yi Qin E;* YSCJ, 258)

> Ever tossed about.
> Many-troubled, many-ailed, my feelings wretched.
> > My feelings wretched.
> > My whole heart muddled;
> > Trying to sort out woe from cheer.

> I'd thought with amused laughter to cast isolation away.
> But I look in the mirror helpless, my face not as before.
> > My face not as before.
> > My talents but shallow,
> > So why is my luck so thin?

Line 2. Singde frequently asserted in verse that his illness stemmed from a passionate nature, for example:

> From ancient times those full of feeling have also many ills. (YSCJ, 332)

> > My life and times like floating cress;
> > My illness brought on from distress. (YSCJ, 307)

Line 10. The Chinese have proverbially believed that, as Li Shangyin put it:

> Since antiquity Talent and one's Lot in life have been at loggerheads. (YSCJ, 258)

Poetic Worlds

TUNE 35, *Song of the South Country (Nan Xiang Zi)*
Inscribed on a Portrait of My Dead Wife (YSCJ, 354)

> I choke back tears, without a sound.
> For the past, I can but rue my callousness.
> Thanks to the portrait, again I recognize . . .
> > Brimming brightly.
> But a sliver of heartache cannot be portrayed.

> > Her parting words are all too clear.
> By midnight, wakened early from a dream of bi-winged birds.
> You, dear, woke early, while I still dream . . .

Watch after watch.
Sobs to exhaustion windy eave-bells in night rain.

Lines 3, 5. Singde adapts two famous lines about the exiled princess, Wang Zhaojun. First he alludes to the third of Du Fu's "Expressing My Feelings about Ancient Sites," in a line Singde interprets:

He recognized in the portrait her spring breeze features.

Then Singde recasts a line from Wang Anshi's "Song of the Radiant Consort":

Airs and grace have never been portrayable in paintings.

Line 7. The bi-winged birds, who share one pair of wings, are a conventional symbol for matrimonial bliss.

By critical consensus, Nalan Singde was the most melancholy poet of his time. Often described as a "man who died for love," he wrote many fine lyrics mourning his wife.[19] In stanza 1, the poet employs paradox to create a more vivid impression of his grief. He sobs without a sound and feels regret for past unfeelingness. His wife's features appear distinctly in her portrait, but their sorrow is unportrayable, yet it is portrayed in Singde's lyric.

In stanza 2, grief seems to have transported the poet to an altered state of consciousness. Is he awake or dreaming, imagining or remembering? Even his wife's dead soul appears lucid and distinct by contrast. Singde concludes by transferring his stricken feelings to the "eave-bells," whose "sobs" give final voice to the grief he choked back.

Critics often write that Nalan Singde was a poet of pure emotion who never gave a thought to allusions or other literary adornments.[20] Singde's ingenious pairing of allusions in *Song of the South Country* belies that characterization. Stanza 1 closes by echoing two poems about Wang Zhaojun, the "Bright Consort" separated by a twist of fate from the emperor who had fallen in love with her portrait. Stanza 2's closing line recalls "Eave-bells in the Misty Rain," a dirge that Tang's Mystic Thearch (r. 712–755) supposedly wrote for his beloved consort, Yang Guifei (see YSCJ, 150, n. 8).

Such subtle resonances between stanzas are hardly the work of a versifier oblivious to the finer points of his craft.

TUNE 36, *As If in a Dream (Ru Meng Ling;* YSCJ, 96)

In a myriad arched yurts, the men are drunk.
Stars' reflections quiver, about to drop.
My homing dream, sundered by Wolf River,
Is then shaken to bits by the river's roar.
Back to sleep!
Back to sleep!
Well I know that in waking there's no savor.

Line 3. The White Wolf River flows east from White Wolf Mountain (near Lingyuan, Liaoning) into the Bohai Sea.

As If in a Dream is famous for its opening strophe, which Wang Guowei called a "magnificent sight for a thousand ages."[21] The lyric is laced with the rhapsodic incoherence of a drunken dream. The spectacle of an entire army intoxicated seems to make the very stars tremble. They quiver and stumble, as if we were viewing them through the eyes of a drunken man. The White Wolf River, "howling" like a drunken horde, dashes the speaker's dream to bits. But the speaker's dazed state makes us wonder, Did he mistake carousing troops for the river's din? Were the stars bobbing in the river? Are those quivering stars a symbol for the "homing dream . . . shaken to bits"? Only one thing remains clear to the speaker, expressed (in the original) by bisyllabic injunctions cadenced like the waves of a river: "Back to sleep! Back to sleep!" That single point of lucidity becomes clearer when we recall that in Chinese "waking" and "sobering up" are expressed by the same word.

TUNE 37, *Song of Golden Threads (Jinlu Qu)*
Sent to Liangfen [Gu Zhenguan] (YSCJ, 478)

Singde's just a mad fellow!
Whose lot, by chance:

grimy dust in the capital,
R aven robes of the mansions.
I sprinkle my wine only on the soil of Zhao;
    But who could appreciate Singde's intent?
Though it's hard to believe, we became best friends.
With flashing eyes we sing out loud, neither of us old;
        Before the cups,
    We've wiped away all our tears for brave men.
        Good sir, don't you see
        The moonlight like water?

Sharing this night, we must get deeply drunk.
        Just let those
        moth-brow slanders fly;
        Then and now, the same jealousy.
The long-troubled course of our lives, no need to ask;
    Put them aside with a cold laugh, and be done!
Worries arise, regrets springing from the very start.
Yet a meeting of hearts for a single day will last 1000 kalpas;
        Future affinities,
    I fear, must be knotted in another life.
        We've taken weighty vows;
        Good sir, don't forget!

Line 3. Singde echoes Lu Ji's (261–303) plaint on the vicissitudes and degradations of capital life:

> In the capital, Loyang, much wind and dust;
> My white robes, transformed to grimy black.

Line 5. Singde quotes a line from Li He's (791–817) "Vast Song." Like Li He, Singde expresses esteem for a discerning patron like Lord Pingyuan, prince of Zhao.

Line 8. When Ruan Ji (210–263), wiliest of Bohemians, received a guest he liked, Ruan's dark eyes would flash. When burdened with an unwanted guest, Ruan would roll the whites of his eyes.

Line 15. Singde alludes to Qu Yuan's lament:

> The crowd is jealous of my moth-brows O!
> They slander me for licentiousness.

Qu Yuan employed moth-brows, a conventional token of feminine beauty, as a symbol for moral excellence.

Line 20. Singde alludes to the friendship of Xiang Liu and Yan Jun (d. 459). When Yan became eminent, he did not try to advance Xiang, but treated him as he always had. Xiang declared:

> Shixun [Yan Jun] and I have long enjoyed a meeting of hearts; how could I [risk that rapport] by dwelling a single day mid wealth and power?[22]

Singde is not known for his "longer tunes," but almost all critics make an exception for this one. Its affirmation of friendship is nobly conceived and graciously expressed. Its powerful first line sweeps away all questions of unequal social status, affirming solidarity with Singde's less fortunate friend. Singde asserts: "Like you, I'm misunderstood; like you, I feel admiring sympathy for heroes out of favor." Stanza 1 closes with an enigmatic figure of "moonlight like water," the only nature image in the entire poem. This image occurs twice elsewhere in Singde's oeuvre, each time helping to create an ethereal, ephemeral atmosphere (YSCJ, III, 340); it recalls a line that Su Shi wrote to his departing friend in a *Joy of Eternal Union:*

> Beneath the tower the full moon's light is like water. (quoted in YSCJ, 479)

Stanza 2 continues to admonish: "Let's get drunk! To hell with slanderers! So what if our stations in life are far apart? Forget about it!" In the third strophe, Singde turns sober and admits regrets for his rash, offbeat behavior. But he quickly finds consolation in asserting that true friendship persists beyond the grave.

The style of *Song of Golden Threads* is truly a tour de force. Singde's powerful subjective rhetoric creates a convincing representation of undying friendship, as the poet runs the elocutionary gamut from exclamation to assertion to rhetorical question to injunction to supposition, before finally binding his friend with a weighty oath of eternal amity.

TUNE 38, *Immortal at the River*
On Winter Willows (YSCJ, 369)

Flying catkins, flying flowers, where have they gone?
    Under layers of ice and ricks of snow, tattered and torn.
Spare and sparse, one tree in the chill of dawn.
      I love its finery in the full moon;
      Even haggard, it draws my concern.

Most of all, when lush threads have fluttered and fallen,
    Yet they remind me of springtime hills.
A skirt-rinsing dream, once snapped, will be hard to mend.
      So much sorrow in the west wind,
      Whose breath cannot uncrease knit brows.

Line 7. The bare willow twigs arch like springtime hills; both can be images of substitution for a woman's eyebrows.[23]

Line 8. Singde alludes to the preface to Li Shangyin's *Willow Twig Lyrics,* in which a maiden proposes to her cousin:

> Three days from now I shall go with some neighbors to rinse our skirts by the river; I'll take my Boshan censer and wait for you there.[24]

Originally a kind of purification rite, "rinsing skirts" later refers to a clandestine tryst.[25]

In praising Singde's "odes on objects," Hu Yunyi points out their distinctive feature: no matter what Singde is describing, in the end his lyrics always seem to express Singde's own feelings.[26] Within this lyric unfolds a world of loss and deterioration. The "barren tree" is a conventional symbol for the talented man who is poorly utilized. Since line 5's fluid syntax enables "haggard" to apply to the speaker as well as to the tree, it is reasonable to interpret the willow as a symbol for such unfortunate gentlemen. In stanza 2, however, the willows are associated with a woman's brows (lines 2 and 5) and skirts. The fiber imagery in "threads," "skirts," "snapped," and "mend" binds willow and woman even closer. On balance, then, we will have to interpret the willow as a symbol for all human misfortune, whether the losses occur in love or in public life.

TUNE 39, *Butterflies Lingering over Flowers*
Going Beyond the Border (YSCJ, 381)

Then and now rivers and mountains have no certain lot.
　　In the painted bugle's cry,
　　　Herd upon herd of horses come and gone.
This view abrim with barren chill, who could express?
The west wind has blown all the scarlet maples old.

Hidden griefs from long ago, where could I find the words?
　　Ironclad steeds, gold-tipped spears,
　　　A green tomb by the road at yellow dusk.
My feelings grow ever deeper, who knows how deep?
Setting sun deep in mountains, rain deep in autumn.

Lines 7–8. Singde alludes first to Xin Qiji's lyric to the tune *Joy of Eternal Union:*

> Gold-tipped spears and ironclad steeds,
> Tigerish esprit bolting a thousand leagues.

Then Singde alludes to Du Fu's lament for the exiled consort Wang Zhaojun, from the third of Du Fu's *Expressing My Thoughts on Ancient Sites:*

> Alone she left behind a green tomb to face the yellow dusk.

Min Zongshu cites an earlier poem about Wang Zhaojun containing the line:[27]

> One song from the lute describes *hidden griefs*.

Quite possibly, the "hidden griefs" belong to Zhaojun as well as to Singde. It is even possible that the young Manchu, mirabile dictu, identified with the exiled Chinese princess!

Line 9. Whenever Huan Yi (d. 392?) heard an a cappella song, he would wail: "What's to be done?" Xie An remarked: Ziye (Huan Yi) certainly is a man whose "feelings grow ever deeper!"[28]

Most traditional critics subscribe to a form of historical determinism that asserts, for example, that only subjects of a robust empire could write magnificent frontier poetry. While I disagree in theory, it is fascinating to note that this border poem, written by the scion of a conquering people, strikes a "mournfully virile and expansive" tone rarely heard in Chinese lyrics since the Tang dynasty.[29] Its first strophe contrasts the uncertain ebb and flow of armies and kingdoms with the eternal presence of rivers and mountains. Strophe 2 turns away from warhorses to describe a barren, hoary border scene; use of the verb-complement construction "blows . . . old" lends mournful line 5 a touch of virility.

Stanza 2 again remarks on the inconstancy of military affairs. Again Singde turns from prancing warhorses to a desolate image of death. But now the first stanza's stirring sounds of blowing bugles, neighing horses, and gusting winds yield to the gentler sad strains of Zhaojun's lute. In the closure, Singde suggests that tragic emotions are as enduring as nature by comparing them to "rain" and "mountains" that recall the opening's eternal "rivers and mountains."

Stylistic features contribute heavily to the lyrical effect. Each strophe begins with overt rhetoric, in the form of a strong assertion or pointed question. It is commonplace in lyrics to repeat the word "deep"; Ouyang Xiu once began a lyric:

Deep, deep lies the little courtyard, who knows how deep?[30]

By belaboring us with four "deeps," Singde overcomes triteness by sheer force of hyperbole.

TUNE 40, *Sand of Silk-washing Stream*
At Mr. Feng's Garden in the West Suburb I Viewed the Crab-apple Blossoms and Was Moved by the Memory of Xiangyan's Lyrics (YSCJ, 129)

Who says that fluttering fall cannot be affecting?
In the season of our old rambles, a skyful of fine flowers.
The brokenhearted one has gone, now for more than a year.

An entire swathe of haloed pink, just touched with rain;
How many threads of pliant willow, now joined with mist.
A lovely spirit seared away before the evening light.

Title. The lyrics of Gong Dingzi, who lived from 1616 to 1673.

Line 5. YSCJ, Hu Yunyi's text, and Huang Tianji's anthology all adopt a different line. But, since the second line in the second stanza of *Sand of Silk-washing Stream must* be parallel, and since every other lyric that Nalan Singde wrote to this tune maintains that parallelism, I have adopted a text variant from the Yueyatang edition mentioned in YSCJ, 129.

Since the crabapple's blossoms are both glorious and short lived, they often inspire Chinese poets to rue the transience of beauty. Singde's ode, as we might expect, keens along at a pretty high pitch, projecting strong emotions from the very first line. Stanza 1 is dominated by sad memories of his departed friend. Stanza 2 describes tender, fragile flowers and catkins touched by the mist and rain that will soon ruin them. Use of the pathetic fallacy in "lovely spirit," as well as the "fluttering fall" from line 1, links the crabapple blossoms' fate with that of the deceased poet, Gong Dingzi.

TUNE 41, *Song of the Wine-fountain (Jiuquan Zi;* YSCJ, III)

Withered is every *tumi* rose.
A swathe of moonlight, bright as water.
Seal incense dispelled,
One remains unsleeping.
Daybreak's crows crying.

In dainty chill, helpless over gauzy robes too thin.
Don't lean by the corner rail.
What saddens one most . . .
The wick about to drop.
Wild geese still flying.

This lyric closely resembles its predecessors from the Five Dynasties. Its bedroom topos, apparently female persona, and boudoir articles such as incense carved with "small seal" graphs, gauzy robes, railings, and guttering candles are all stock elements in the tenth-century anthology *Among the Flowers*. Singde's heroine, disturbed by the dying last blossoms of spring and by the aqueous moonlight, is deprived of her beauty sleep. Chilly and alone, she gazes outside, toward her absent lover. The last lines in both stanzas recall part of Wen Tingyun's *Song of the Water-clock:*

> Startling frontier-pass geese,
> Rousing the city-wall crows.[31]

The crows in both lyrics provoke the neglected wife to think of the wider world beyond her boudoir. The migrant geese provide a painful reminder that her sojourner has strayed far from their nighttime roost.

With considerable justification, Singde's lyrics have been criticized for exploring only a narrow range of poetic worlds.[32] Nearly all Singde's 344 lyrics are dominated by an expressive component, as the speaker pours out his or her "powerful, spontaneous emotions."[33] As Hu Yunyi describes it, Singde's lyric oeuvre "contains no lofty, profound thought or abstruse philosophical speculation, but merely the throbbing of addled, lovesick feelings."[34]

We may divide Singde's lyrics into six categories, based on theme and content: elegies, poems on parting, frontier poems, poems on friendship, odes on objects, and poems about frustrated passion. Lyrics from the first group (such as YSCJ, 354, tune 35 above) are dominated by an overwhelming sense of grief and loss evoked by contrasts between past and present. Thus, in one elegy the bereaved poet describes bygone happy days with his wife, then concludes with the exclamation:

> Back then we called these merely routine! (YSCJ, 124)

Lyrics lamenting departure (e.g., tune 40 above) closely resemble the elegies; they, too, are pervaded by memory, loss, and powerful anguish. The frontier songs (see tunes 36 and 39 above) are distinguished, as William Schultz has observed, by their "Chinese" attitude.[35] Instead of evoking a Manchu pride in martial prowess and the rugged outdoor life, frontiers always make Singde yearn for the comforts of hearth and home, as in the following example:

> A watch of wind.
> A watch of snow,
> Dinning to bits my homeward heart and dreams that won't come true.
> My old garden had no such noise. (YSCJ, 105)

Singde, like most Chinese literati, left a sizable corpus of occasional poetry written to friends. Singde's is distinguished by its prevalence of propositional language and by his customary emotional intensity (see tune 37 above). Singde also wrote several odes on objects (e.g., tune 38 above); here, again, Singde's are characterized by prominence of self-expressive elements. Thus, in describing snowflakes, Singde declares:

> These are not rich and honored blossoms of the human world,
> (YSCJ, 224)

a line that subsequent Chinese critics have used to describe Singde's own character.[36]

The last category is a catchall, comprised of all the lyrics dealing with passion, especially with frustrated love. Most of these are set in boudoirs and differ from earlier models chiefly by the candor and vehemence with which the heroine expresses her sorrows. Hu Yunyi has sagely observed that Singde is very much a "courtier-poet" singing of capital life and of tender sentiments within palace apartments; what sets Singde's "court poetry" apart is the thick pall of woe and suffering that suffuses it.[37]

Language

The salient characteristic of Singde's verbal art is its relatively unadorned style. Hu calls this the "plain sketch" technique, in which scenes and events are outlined with just a few strokes; what images remain serve to mirror and express the speaker's state of mind.[38] The images that Singde commonly depicts are those of the boudoir and garden. He is particularly fond of nocturnal imagery, such as moonlight and dreams. Singde often (about ten times) contrasts the full moon with "waning" in human affairs, for example:

> I rather suspect the moon insists on being full tonight. (YSCJ, 154, at the end of an ode to an absent lover)

> Uncomprehending our longings, moonlight brims full tonight. (YSCJ, 453, end)

>> Where to express these longings?
>> Vainly remains the moon from that time.
>> But the moon, too, has changed from back then.
>> Roundly it reflects my silken sidelocks. (YSCJ, 181, end)

It is tempting to compare Singde's dream imagery with that of Keats. Singde's dreams, too, are apt to contrast blissful illusion with wretched consciousness. The exaltation of drunken dreams in *As If in a Dream,* for example, recalls the "Ode to a Nightingale." The speaker's disillusioned awakening recalls Madeline's despair in "The Eve of St. Agnes":

>> No dream, alas! alas! and woe is mine!

Although Singde's poems do not associate dreams with creative imagination, he yearns with equal passion for those fleeting visions:

> Even in dreams it was none too clear.
> Then why must they spur my dreams awake? (YSCJ, 285, end)

>> Don't laugh that our lives are but a dream;
>> A good dream turns out to be so rare. (YSCJ, 304)

>> Dimly recalled, our lovers' tryst is truly like a dream;
>> Were it so, let me dream on! (YSCJ, 303, end)

One frequent word at the beginning of Singde's lyrics is "soak/ sodden." At least a dozen lyrics open with a sodden scene evocative of dismal tears, for example:

Sodden clouds have pressed down all the several peaks. (YSCJ, 106, line 1)

Sunset rains, thread upon thread, blow soddenly. (YSCJ, 110, line 1)

> Pinkish shadows soak the secluded casement.
> Emaciating the springtime light. (YSCJ, 306, lines 1-2)

It is only fair to keep in mind the grander side to Singde's imagery. Though most of his frontier poetry presents a remarkably "dainty and oblique" atmosphere, some of his border images are of the powerful and unrestrained variety:[39]

We'll shoot a dragon mid wind and rain, drive on the hundred spirits. (YSCJ, 81)

A myriad leagues of the west wind over the Gobi sands. (YSCJ, 224, end)

As a rule, however, Singde's imagery is more introverted and more rueful. Huang Tianji has calculated, for example, that "woe" occurs ninety times in Singde's lyrics, while "tears" fall sixty-five times, and "sorrow" darkens nearly forty lines.[40]

When Singde does not employ the "plain sketch" technique, he uses quite a few compound images. He is wont to liken a variety of tangible objects to dreams, as in:

> Dense flowers, like a dream. (YSCJ, 318)

Other notable similes include:

My grief like tides of day and night along the Xiang River. (YSCJ, 89)

The silken strands of rain like dust, as clouds bear water. (YSCJ, 364)

Singde's numerous images of substitution nearly always serve to invest concrete objects with the poet's melancholy mood. Almost any number of things are credited with tears, for example:

Rain ceases, the phoenix-tree's tears soon stop. (YSCJ, 128)

By my pillow, the red ice is thin. (YSCJ, 186)

(The missing tenors here are frozen "tears of blood" in a wintry room.)

How many red waxen tears have dripped away?
When will they dry? (YSCJ, 274, end)

(Tears are a conventional image of substitution for a candle's drippings.) The conceit that strong emotions can consume us like a candle generates the following figures of "heart-ash":

The heart's ashes consumed. (YSCJ, 70, line 1)

Purple Jade stirs the chilly ash:
The "heart" graphs all gone. (YSCJ, 305)

(On one kind of incense was impressed the graph for "heart.")

My heart's former feelings are now ash. (YSCJ, 406)

Singde's use of transference usually conveys a similarly somber burden, for example:

The East wind doesn't understand woe. (YSCJ, 112)

The crystal curtain a swathe of heart-wounding white. (YSCJ, 200, line 1)

The West wind sobs at night. (YSCJ, 237)

Why again, as night deepens the clear dew,
Do [flowers] weep sad pinks? (YSCJ, 294, end)

If we had to ascribe a flavor to Singde's poetry, it would be a
bitter one. Indeed, Singde uses the word "savor" seven times,
always modified by sorrow, desolation, or loneliness, for example:

Let it brew forth all the savor of lonesome sleep. (YSCJ, 359)

On what day will you return,
That we may sample together
The savor of night rain on the empty steps? (YSCJ, 445, end)

Another way in which Singde animates objects is by the verbal
complement "ruin," which occurs at least ten times, for example:

During the night she grieved her tiny waist to ruins. (YSCJ, 133)

Teardrops hard to dispel:
Lengths of jade dripping the grayish mist to ruins. (YSCJ, 207)

Having rubbed to ruins Wu damask
And cried to tatters Shu paper. (YSCJ, 511)

In all these examples of transference, nature appears transformed
by the poet's mood or, to borrow Hu Yunyi's term, "melancho-
lized."[41]

Even a cursory reading of Singde's lyrics reveals a preponderance of modal language and "hypotatic" syntax.[42] I would esti-
mate that nearly half the lyrics in Singde's oeuvre contain at least
one stanza dominated by strong subjective rhetoric. Dozens of
lyrics begin and end as overtly as this one:

How could I remain silent and lonely in this season of
fragrant growth? . . .
Don't ask after fame that lasts a thousand, myriad years. (YSCJ,
217)

Often, Singde weds colloquial speech to his overt rhetorical style, creating vivid impressions of direct speech, for example:

> Is it she who was unlucky?
> Is it I who was callous?
> Hard to believe more wearing down could have made it better?
> Was it necessary for the chilly water-clock to hasten us on? (YSCJ, 342)

(According to Chinese proverb, "for a good thing, much wearing down" is necessary.)

> With the hint of a scold she feigns a sneer:
> "If ye weren't so forlorn,
> Would ye have come, now?" (YSCJ, 292)

It gives us some idea of Singde's insistently questioning tone to consider that "Who?" occurs no fewer than ninety-two times in his lyrics, for example:

> Who says the Shadow Mountain road is hard to travel? (YSCJ, 316, line 1)

> Regrets for my life and times, with whom could I speak? (YSCJ, 489)

> Really,
>> for whom does she grow sicker?
>> And for whom is she so shy? (YSCJ, 306)

Nor does this statistic fully convey the ubiquity of Singde's rhetorical questions, for we yet have to count "what," "when," "where," "why," and "how."

Singde is a master at lending drama or even melodrama to expressions of emotion.[43] One important way that Singde achieves dramatic intensity is by uttering paradoxical statements:

> When we're filled with passion, our passions seem slight. (YSCJ, 273)

Is it callousness, or is it sorrow? (YSCJ, 313)

I nearly laughed at myself from surfeit of sorrow;
Why now do I bite back tears from an excess of joy? (YSCJ, 277)

Du Mu deserves at least a nod of acknowledgment here, for underlying all these paradoxes is Du's famous line:

Great passion seems like no passion at all.

Singde, however, deserves credit for some highly ingenious and evocative variations on Du Mu's theme.

Singde pours out his feelings so often that he is forced to go to extremes in order to keep his presentation forceful and fresh. His dexterity with these subjective rhetorical figures constitutes his chief stylistic contribution to the verbal art of the Chinese lyric.

Due to Singde's frank, explicit style, Chinese critics have tended to view him as an untutored genius whose lyrics simply sprang pristinely from his head, unsullied by allusions, revisions, or any sort of conscious artistry.[44] To borrow Alan Tormey's terms, these critics have confused the effect of a poet's "style of performance" with the workings of his creative process.[45] Actually, Singde was anything but naive about the Chinese poetic tradition, and the extent of his lore can be measured by the high frequency of allusions in his verse.

Nearly all Singde's quotations and allusive references are to earlier poetry. The bulk are to the conventional furniture of lyric poetry: rinsing skirts, trimming the wicks together, lighting censers from Boshan, and the like. The examples cited all derive from Li Shangyin's poetry, to which Singde owes an enormous debt. Singde quotes or paraphrases lines from Li Shangyin's verse on at least a hundred occasions; among the more significant borrowings are:

The ornamented year's burgeoning flows after the water. (YSCJ, 169, line 1)

This feeling had already become a memory to be cherished. (YSCJ, 230)[46]

Surely it will share a branch with Han Ping.[47]
In the chilly night, an expanse of ice before the pillow. (YSCJ, 307; a note gives the source line in Li's oeuvre)

As we can see from the quoted examples, Singde usually alludes to Li Shangyin's verse to reinforce a sense of frustrated love. Li Shangyin is most famous for precisely his poems that "emphasize the anguish of hopeless yet unrelenting love."[48] We might even accuse Singde's whole oeuvre of being a set of allusive variations on Li's work. Aside from the extensive verbal borrowings, Singde explores just those realms of passion "so intense and all-consuming that it becomes self-destructive and often arouses thoughts of death."[49]

One further proof of Singde's debt is that the poet whom Singde quotes second most often in his lyrics, Wang Cihui (1593?–1642?), is best known for modern-style *shi* filled with erotic decor and unorthodox passions, quite in Li Shangyin's style.[50] Among dozens of examples, we may cite:

A waning moon furtively peeps at the gold doorknocker. (YSCJ, 136)[51]
All who have passions can fulfill their prayers. (YSCJ, 165; a note provides the source line by Wang Cihui)

Naturally, Singde often borrows or adapts lines by earlier lyricists, especially those from the Five Dynasties and the northern Soong. Singde's favorite sources are Wei Zhuang, Yan Shu, and Yan Shu's son, Yan Jidao, for example:

Where to speak of longings?
Vainly remains the moon from back then. (YSCJ, 181)[52]

Even in dreams, when did I ever reach Xie's Bridge? (YSCJ, 220)[53]

Nowadays I've grown afraid to mention affairs from back then;
I've knotted a bosomful of orchids.
Moonlight fades, lamplight deepens.
In a dream the Cloud returns, where can I find her? (YSCJ, 232)[54]

Unsurprisingly, Singde occasionally quotes from operatic dramas of the Yuan and Ming that affirm love's all-conquering power, works such as *Romance of the West Chamber* and *The Peony Pavilion*. The following quotation from Bai Pu's *Autumn Night Rain on the Phoenix Trees* is a perfect example of the kind of lines that Singde preferred to borrow:

> Passionate twigs and sorrowing leaves. (YSCJ, 435)

Singde paid careful attention to the prosody of his shorter tunes. He was known to be a fine zitherer, had a hand in producing a prosodic manual entitled *A Correct Compendium of Lyric Rhymes,* and wrote at least six new lyric tunes himself.[55] Appropriately enough, one of the tunes is entitled *Tear-stained Blue Blouse* (YSCJ, 278). Curiously, Singde did not lavish the same care on his adagios, which have been criticized for shoddy prosody.[55] Such liberties appear to result from Singde's identification with the aesthetics of the "literati lyric" rather than from an insensitivity to musical effects. Singde makes frequent and effective use of binomes for musical and emotional effects. The most common is a cluster of binomes beginning with *qi* ("forlorn"), such as *qiliang* ("forlorn and desolate," twenty-one occurrences), *qimi* ("lost and forlorn," five occurrences), and *qiqie* ("intensely forlorn," four occurrences), for example:

> After all, for whom am I desolately forlorn? (YSCJ, 249, end)

> Limitlessly lost and forlorn! (YSCJ, 305, end)

Another prolific cluster of binomes begins with *ji* ("silent"), such as *jimo* ("silent and lonesome," ten occurrences; in Ancient Chinese, *jimo* was a rhyming binome: *dz'iek mak*), *jiji* ("silent and unheard"), and *jiliao* ("silent and deserted"), for example:

How can I remain silent and lonely in a season of fragrant growth? (YSCJ, 217, line 1)

When southern geese have flown back home, it's even more silent and deserted. (YSCJ, 215, end)

Another common cluster of binomes is *xiaoxiao* ("desolate soughing") and its relatives *xiaosuo, xiaoshu,* and so on, which occur about thirty times, including:

> The wind sighs desolately,
> The rain soughs desolately. (YSCJ, 220)

The frequent appearance of such binomes contributes much to the doleful tenor of Singde's verse.

Conclusion

Both in his poetry and in his writings about literature, Singde reveals his belief that literature is an expression of "native sensibility."[56] In assessing Singde's place in literary history, it is only natural to compare him with lyricists who express emotions candidly and straightforwardly. The lyrics of Wei Zhuang, for example, are renowned for venting feelings and recollections of love in a "straightforward . . . direct . . . hypotactic way."[57] Wei's innovative use of colloquial language and explicit rhetoric exerted a strong influence on Singde, as Singde's frequent allusions to Wei's lyrics suggest.[58] On the other hand, Singde's lyrics are more distraught, even more feeling oriented, and less image oriented than those by Wei Zhuang.

Perhaps the lyric oeuvre of Li Yu would make a better object for comparison. After all, a key difference between Li Yu and Wei Zhuang is that the former's lyrics are even more explicit, more intensely personal than Wei's.[59] The majority view among Chinese critics has been that Singde, in Chen Weisong's words, "captured the legacy of the Two Rulers of the Southern Tang."[60]

Indeed, Singde learned much from Li Yu; Li's use of minimalist "plain sketch," his ability to "make concrete images stand for the various shades of his emotions," and his air of "unaffected sincerity" all resonate in Singde's lyrics, too.[61] What distinguishes Li Yu's later lyrics from Singde's is the breadth and depth of their emotional appeal. Singde, too, can gush out personal sorrows at the drop of a hat and not infrequently bursts into a general lament on the sorrows of human existence. Yet rarely does he convince us that his personal sufferings mirror those of all men. Although Singde writes no less poignantly than Li Yu, we would not say of Singde, as critics have written of Li Yu, that "the individual sorrow expressed in his lyrics seems to express all human suffering, just as Jesus and Buddha bore by themselves the weight of all human sin."[62]

Even closer parallels can be drawn between the verse of Singde and that of Yan Jidao (1030?–1106?). Yan, too, experienced the privileges of a young aristocrat, and his lyrics expose the hollowness of that life. Zheng Qian has remarked of Yan's lyrics that "above the ornate and gorgeous decor hangs a pall of dark depression."[63] Chen Tingzhuo remarked that "Yan excels at expressing feelings"; like Singde, Yan often explores tangled worlds of emotion, such as:

> If you ask when wanting you will cease.
> When I see you, wanting you will end . . .
> Yet in wanting to see you, I tell all about wanting you.[64]

The type of poetic closure that we have seen in Singde's verse often reminds us strongly of Yan's conclusions, like:

> The winestains on my robe and the words within my verse;
> Blot after blot and line after line,
> Every one spells my forlorn desolation!
> The red candle pities itself for having no good plan.
> In the late night chill, it vainly weeps for me.[65]

Yan's verse is so pervaded by grief that critics dubbed him one of "the most heart-broken men in history."[66] We can detect traces of his style in Singde's work. For example, Yan's trademark is to pair red (flowers) and green (growth) and then imbue them with an unexpectedly melancholy cast.[67] Singde employs the same technique on numerous occasions, notably:

> Rouged tears by the green window. (YSCJ, 278)

> Rueful reds and sorrowing greens. (YSCJ, 498)

But the similarity between the two poets depends less on Singde's verbal debt than on the atmosphere common to their lyrics, for Yan and Singde seem to have been very much kindred spirits. Singde's good friend Gu Zhenguan implied this when he praised Singde:

> With his pedigree and talent, he bids fair to surpass Yan [Jidao]![68]

To this day, Singde remains the most popular Qing lyricist. Among critics who share that admiration is Wang Guowei, who hailed Singde as "the one and only great lyricist since the Northern Soong."[69] Wang attributes Singde's achievement to his pristine innocence, averring that, "since he had just entered China and was not imbued with the Han people's customs, his lyrics were able to achieve such unaffected intensity."[70] Hu Yunyi, too, sees Singde as something of a noble savage, a pure breath of Manchu air sweeping away the stale classicism that was choking Chinese lyricism.[71] While Wang and Hu are certainly exaggerating, it *is* tempting to cast Singde as Mozart against Zhu Yizun's Salieri.

Still, Singde is not without his detractors. Chen Tingzhuo, who criticized Yan Jidao for a narrow preoccupation with love to the exclusion of more "proper" and elevated concerns, also criticizes Singde for being "shallow and obvious."[72] Chen Tui's criticism of Singde is more incisive: "A thousand pieces, all to the same tune."[73] My own assessment is that Singde's oeuvre is indeed narrow and rather monotonous but that he displays genius precisely where Zhu Yizun flagged—in the powerful presentation of his own inner life. For this achievement, Singde should be awarded no lower a place in Qing poetry than his erudite friend.

Conclusion

Thus far we have been concerned with each lyricist's distinctive contributions to the genre. Chen Zilong we found to be a minor lyricist of limited range, yet one whose lyrics reveal beauty and the potential power of implicit emotions. Wu Weiye displayed greater variety in his poetic worlds, from racy sensuality to travel descriptions to grander explorations of historical time and personal fate. Since his verbal art is relatively undistinguished, however, Wu's lyrical achievements are no greater than those of Chen Zilong. Wang Fuzhi we found to be the most underrated of the six poets. He explores many different poetic realms, from simple parables about ginger and marionettes to complex examinations of beauty, legend, and loss. Wang's poetic language, too, is refreshingly diverse; in his verse we may hear anything from the colloquial strains of a street vendor to the erudite intonements of a classical scholar. Traditional critics condemn Wang's prosodic deficiencies, but this imbalance between poetic and musical qualities is not apparent in translation. Wang Fuzhi must be considered an important lyricist.

Chen Weisong (Qinian), on the other hand, has been overrated by his supporters. To be sure, Qinian has created some superb lyrics in a variety of styles, and in reviving the "powerful and unrestrained" mode he conveys an unprecedented measure of affective power. But Qinian's appealing bluster masks a lack of intellectual depth and a certain monotony of language. Though Qinian was an influential figure in the subsequent development of

Qing lyrics, his verse does not quite match up to that of Wang Fuzhi. It is rather the lyric oeuvre of Qinian's friend, Zhu Yizun, that meets the criteria for important poetry; it displays mastery of form, variety of content, and elegance of style. Zhu revived the "subtle and sophisticated" style of Zhou Bangyan and his southern Soong heirs, but Zhu's lyrics avoid their "opaque," "veiled" quality.[1] Except for a bookish flavor that some readers find distasteful, Zhu's oeuvre is nearly flawless. If only he displayed a bit less learning and a bit more inspiration, Zhu would be a truly great lyricist.

For such inspiration, we must turn to that fascinating artistic prodigy, Nalan Singde. Rather like Mozart's earlier music, Singde's works amaze us at first with their seemingly artless, effortless grace, then amaze us again when we perceive the masterly technique and skilled craftsmanship creating that impression of spontaneous genius. Although Singde explored only a narrow range of poetic worlds and made only limited contributions to the verbal art of the lyric, his revival of the mournfully explicit style of Li Yu and Yan Jidao enriched Qing verse. Singde's best efforts achieve a penetrating psychological insight and a powerful, poignant expressiveness that perfectly complement Zhu Yizun's oeuvre. The young Manchu deserves equal status with his friend, the erudite "Salieri."

Such subtle distinctions should not blind us to the considerable similarities between the six literati. All exhibited a preoccupation with the scars of the Ming collapse, a concern for "elevating" the lyric form, and a scholarly emphasis on learned tradition at the expense of native inspiration. From the "old country" haunting Chen Zilong's lyrics to Singde's elegies on the Ming tombs, all six poets wrote at least a few lyrics expressing or implying sorrow at the tragic events of the mid-seventeenth century. From Chen Zilong's avoidance of boudoir poetry to Wang Fuzhi's allegorizing to Singde's enhancement of the lyric's pedigree:

The lyric's origins far surpass those of *shi*-poems' prosody;
It's modelled on music archive ballads, with a few embellishments,[2]

we detect a continuous attempt to raise the lyric's focus from the trivial and decadent to the serious and refined. Finally, each poet wrote by imitating past models and by weaving together allusions, motifs, and themes common to the genre. Chen Zilong's lyrics may seem relatively free from allusion, but they are redolent with derivations from Five Dynasties lyrics. Though Wang Fuzhi's verse is refreshingly free of lyrical topoi, he just replaces them with the language and conventions of earlier *shi* poetry. Even Singde's lyrics, which are hailed for clearing the stuffy, pedantic air of early Qing verse with a display of "native sensibility," are packed with references to the poetry of Li Shangyin and early lyricists. Our six lyricists, like all Qing literati, staggered under a burden of the literary past that would make even Harold Bloom blanch.

In selecting six exemplary lyricists, I do not mean to imply that no other seventeenth-century writers could produce fine lyrics. One who did was Li Wen (1608–1647), who was Chen Zilong's best friend in the 1630s. Ironically, Li Wen, who drafted proclamations for the Shunzhi emperor, became the first southerner to hold high office in the Manchu government.[3] Oddly enough, Li Wen died early from illness just a few months before Chen Zilong committed suicide. Although few Qing scholars esteemed the poetry of a man who had served two masters, one critic did opine that Li Wen,

> while unable to match [Zilong] for subtle resonances retained within strikingly novel coinages, did surpass [Zilong] in expressive talent.[4]

The following is a typical example of Li Wen's style:

TUNE 42, *Deva-like Barbarian*
Thinking of One Who Hasn't Arrived[5]

Before the rose has rinsed off rouged rain.
The east wind should not hasten him away.

Matters of the heart, unclear to us both.
A Jade Syrinx midst springtime dreams.

In sunset light, veiled by fragrant grass.
Gaze abrim with heartbreaking emerald.
Mutely, I ask of the green hills.
The green hills echo a cuckoo's call.

Line 4. Jade Syrinx was an unlucky maiden in love; she starved herself when her lover failed to keep a seven-year tryst.

Li Wen clearly writes in the same vein as his friend, Chen Zilong—short tunes filled with flowers, grass, and broken hearts. Not only does Li's lyric feature rouged rain and a cuckoo's call, but it also shares an adversative relation with nature. Just as Chen's lyrics are likely to rail at swallows or at the east wind, here nature's tearful rain, heartbreaking greenery, and the cuckoo's doleful response torment the speaker who is ready, like Jade Syrinx, to "die for love."

Wang Shizhen is the most important early Qing lyricist not to warrant his own chapter. The most famous *shi* poet of the early Qing, Wang's willingness to experiment with the lyric greatly boosted its popularity (see above). One scholar even awarded Wang the dubious distinction of asserting that the early Qing lyric's "base and decadent" tone was due to Wang's influence.[6] More charitable critics hail Wang's short tunes for exemplifying the qualities he stressed in his literary theory—"intuitive apprehension of reality, intuitive artistry, and an ineffable personal tone."[7] While Wang's poetic fame seems to have inflated early assessments of his lyrics, some of his short tunes contain delicate, delightful excursions into familiar worlds of love and loss in which the influence of Chen Zilong and Wu Weiye is perceptible.[8]

TUNE 43, *Sands of Silk-washing Stream*
Written at Redbridge [northwest of Yangzhou], in the Company of Zhouan [Yuan Yuling], Chacun [Du Jun], Qinian [Chen Weisong], and Qiuyai [Cao Yue][9]

Past north rampart, Blue Stream ribbonlike flows.
Redbridge's scenery, autumnal before my eyes.
Green poplars by the city-wall; that's Yangzhou!

Gazing west toward Thunder Pond, where is it now?
Fragrant souls scattered and lost still sadden us.
Faint mist and fragrant grasses: the old Maze Hall.

Line 4. Thunder Pond is the site of the tomb of Sui's Fiery Thearch (r. 605–616).

Line 6. Maze Hall was the Fiery Thearch's southern palace. It was so cunningly constructed, on so grand a scale, that people often got lost inside for as much as a day.

This lyric was famous in its day; its rhymes were harmonized by dozens of poets, including Nalan Singde (YSCJ, 145). It illustrates the affinities between Shizhen's lyrics and modern-style *shi* poetry. Lin Shuenfu has argued that the structure of *Sands of Silk-washing Stream* approximates that of a regulated verse, with line 3 corresponding to the second couplet of a regulated verse and line 6 bearing the whole weight of a concluding couplet.[10] Since line 3 in lyrics to this tune effects a semiclosure, I would rather compare its structure to a "double quatrain." Line 3 of Shizheng's lyric certainly would make a fine closure for a descriptive quatrain. It not only carries the rhetorical force of assertion but also takes our eyes beyond the visible scene, beyond the confines of the stanza. This type of conclusion is in fact common in Tang and Soong quatrains, for example:

Now I gaze back at Bingzhou; *that's* my homeland![11]

A lone cloud in the setting sun; *that's* Chang'an![12]

As Kao Yu-kung and Mei Tsu-lin have pointed out, such examples convey strong emotions and transcend the quatrain's boundaries by pointing toward a cherished object that is actually beyond reach.[13]

The mood of yearning deepens in stanza 2, as "there's Yangzhou!" gives way to "where's Thunder Pond?" "Scattered and lost," "faint mist," and "maze" all suggest that splendors of the past are irrevocably buried. Although the last line lacks a copula, its implicit equation of palace ruins with mist and weeds parallels the last line in stanza 1, accentuating the antithesis between past and present that so troubles Wang Shizhen.[14]

TUNE 44, *Butterflies Lingering over Flowers*
Harmonizing with the *Jade-washing Lyrics* [of Li Qingzhao][15]

The chilly night sinks deeply, the ornate clepsydra freezes.
    Sprawled on my pillow, sleepless;
        Now I hear the country cocks stir.
At this moment, a groundless ennui you're not here to share;
Moonlight traverses a window-seam, spring chill is oppressive.

Recall when we so seamlessly shared a brocade quilt.
    You seemed the flower of the phoenix-tree,
        And I seemed the phoenix-tree's "phoenix."
Bygone affairs from faraway vainly intrude my dreams.
A silvery *koto* faltering plays the "Strung Pearls" gigue.

Line 8. The *wutong* is sometimes called the "phoenix-tree," for it is believed to be the only tree on which the legendary phoenix would alight. The "phoenix-tree phoenix" is a kind of parakeet, which is said to sup the morning dew from phoenix-tree flowers.

A second characteristic of Wang Shizhen's verse is his fondness for boudoir lyrics of the tenth century. Since these were among the earliest literati lyrics, imitating them acquired a special cachet in the eyes of antiquarian Qing literati. In this poem, Shizhen employs the female persona and the furnishings appropriate for the bedroom topos. The frozen clepsydra conveys not only the chill, but also the endlessness, of a night spent alone; each interval between drops drags on so long that time itself seems to have frozen. Nor does line 3 herald the onset of dawn, for "country cocks" are supposed to cry in the middle of the night.

In stanza 2, the heroine escapes for a moment to the comforts of memory. "Seamlessly" and the shared quilt's warmth transform the closing from stanza 1. In dreams, she can recall birds and flowers, otherwise conspicuously absent from this springtime ode. The concluding music perfectly evokes the heroine's sentiments. She may once have played or danced to this gay tune for her lover, but now the song falters, and the "strung pearls" remind her only of teardrops or of frozen drops of time.

Cao Zhenji (1634–?) was one of the most popular lyricists of his day.[16] Often associated with Zhu Yizun's West Zhejiang school, Cao befriended both Zhu and Chen Weisong. Critics are united in praising Cao's "orthodox elegance."[17] Cao's attitude toward the lyric was relatively original and high minded; he espoused turning one's back on the ancients in order to accord with them and declined to write boudoir poetry.[18] Cao's best lyrics are "odes on objects" written in the manner of Wang Yisun and Zhang Yan:[19]

TUNE 45, *Detaining the Guest (Liu Ke Zhu)*
On Partridges[20]

Miasmic mists bitter!
Everywhere on five streams,
On sands bright and waters indigo,
Call after call, unceasing;
All beseeching the traveler not to leave.
Travelers then and now like shuttles weave;
Why should they care any more
For the constant chatter you convey?
A vacant temple, a ruined post-house;
Though
the sojourner's blouse is drenched,
Horse's hooves are hard put to halt.

Wind and then rain.
A single wisp of the Central Plain
Vanished, no vantage point.
Myriad leagues of torrid wasteland:

Let it
        tear and tatter your feathers.
Do you recall
        the King of Yue's spring palace,
        Palace ladies like blossoms;
      But nowadays only you remain.
        The cuckoo's cry continues;
I imagine
        the river deepen, the moon grow black,
        As Servitor Fu lowers his head.

Line 2. The Five Streams lie west of Grotto Court Lake, near modern Yuanling, Hunan.

Line 13. This recalls lines written by Su Shi when he was exiled on Hainan Island:

    Nearly vanished, where the sky lowers and the falcon plunged,
    A single wisp of green hill—that's the Central Plain![21]

Lines 17–19. These lines allude to Li Bai's celebrated *Viewing an Ancient Site in Yue:*

    After conquering Wu, the King of Yue returned in triumph;
    All his chivalrous warriors were clad in silk on coming home.
    The court ladies, like blossoms, filled the palace in spring,
    Where now only a few partridges are flying about.[22]

Line 22. "Servitor Fu" is Du Fu, who referred to himself in that way in his poem *Northern Journey:*

        The Eastern Alien rebellion still isn't over;
        Servitor Fu's indignation presses keenly.[23]

Cao's "ode on an object" cleverly uses the tune title's underlying meaning, for these partridges are singing an exile's lament, and the Chinese word for "guest" also means "exile." The partridge's cry is popularly thought to sound like "Don't go, brother," and stanza 1 is dominated by its persistent cry. The partridges ubiquitously, endlessly urge traveler-exiles not to leave the south. Only in the stanza's last line do we see that the constant chatter is unavailing, that the "guest" will not be detained.

In stanza 2, the partridge becomes a symbol of the exile. In a fragmented world whose "center cannot hold," only the partridge persists. Its opposite number, the cuckoo, urges "Why not go home?" but the conclusion raises barriers of water and blackness that doom the loyal exile to indefinite banishment. Cao has been attacked for his closing allusion, which some critics feel is too plainspokenly pedantic and deficient in lingering "tone."[24] Actually, the reference to Du Fu as loyal minister away from court is appropriate. The penultimate line also echoes the language of Du Fu's first "Dream of Li Bai," in which Du Fu fears for the safety of his exiled friend:

> Your spirit went back, the mountain pass blackened . . .
> The river is deep, the waves are vasty.[25]

Cao's pairing of the dangers of a lost soul's flight with the persistence of a loyal heart's concern is not at all bad. Du Fu's northern flight and Li's southern exile provide apt parallels for this exile in the south. It is, however, typical of Zhu Yizun's "West Zhejiang" adherents to spread allusions on a bit thickly at times.

One last early Qing lyricist of note was Singde's good friend, Gu Zhenguan (1637–1714). Gu is best remembered for two quite epistolary lyrics written to the unfortunate exile, Wu Zhaoqian.[26] Gu writes in a powerful and unrestrained style; as Chen Tingzhuo remarks, Gu's lyrics "triumph entirely with emotions."[27] Gu was strongly influenced by Xin Qiji and often employed proselike diction in his lyrics, even using the lyric form to write colophons and elegies as well as epistles:[28]

TUNE 46, *Sailing at Night (Ye Xing Chuan)*
Atop Lush, Lone Pavilion [on Helan Mountain, Jiangxi][29]

Let me ask this lush and lonely alp:
Who comes here, on snowy days and moonlit nights?
  The Five Ranges of Viet spanning the south,
  The Seven Realms of Min crouch in the east;
For all time, "Rivers and Mountains like a scroll."

A hundred cares, vast and vague, converge here.
Indifferent to going home, as the setting sun hangs in the west.
  So many heroic sentiments,
  Such unprovoked traveler's tears,
 As the Eighteen Rapids flow downstream.

Line 5. Gu alludes to Su Shi's famous lyric "Recalling Antiquity at Red Cliff" and to Xin Qiji's celebrated couplet:

> Below Lush, Lone Pavilion, the clear river's flow.
> Within it, how many traveler's tears?[30]

Another name for "Lush, Lone Pavilion" is "Pylon-gazing Terrace," commemorating loyal officials in exile who would gaze toward the pylons of the Imperial City gate. Surrounded in his mind's eye by all the great mountains of the south, the poet contrasts their eternal fortitude with men's uncertain loyalties. But, in stanza 2, the poet declares himself to be of loyal nature. The teeming objects of his concern expand as vastly as the landscape before him. Though he is "serenely indifferent" to the rewards of official service, thoughts of his country and the distant "capital pylons" still provoke exile's tears, even as the setting sun and flowing waters suggest the vanity of all human endeavors.

The stylistic trait that distinguishes this lyric is its proselike diction. The first line in each stanza employs a classical Chinese particle more common in essays than in lyrics. "Let me ask," "Who comes," "Serenely indifferent to going home," "So many," and "Such unprovoked" are all redolent of classical prose.

These represent just the finest early Qing lyricists, for in no age was more lyric poetry written. In terms of quality, however, few seventeenth-century lyricists could even equal, let alone surpass, their Soong predecessors. One reason was that Qing poets, in Lin Meiyi's draftsman's metaphor, "could not escape their predecessors' square and rule."[31] Qing writers were largely content to imitate their favorite poets. With the different values they placed on convention and invention, Qing lyricists found originality less important than the "celebration of continuity."[32] To Western readers, this seems to imbalance tradition and the individual talent, and, even in Chinese literary history, the Qing stands out as an age in which talent *(cai)* was subordinated to learning *(xue)*.[33]

It is ironic that Qing poets imitated Soong lyrical diction so closely. It was the very inclusion of fresh colloquialisms that had made the lyric so vivid and supple in the first place. But Qing lyricists, writing in a literary language leavened with fossilized colloquialisms five hundred years old, had strayed far from that heterogeneous style. Their very faithfulness to the letter of Soong diction meant a betrayal of its spirit. They failed to heed dramatist Li Yu's (1611–1685) warning that the lyric must rid itself of three personalities: the neo-Confucian moralist, the Zen monk, and the pedant.[34] Qing lyricism certainly suffered from its failure to subdue scholasticism.

Another cause cited for the defects of seventeenth-century lyrics is the dampening influence of tyranny. Wang Jiyou has argued that literati were too cowed to display their "talent and spirit" and so took refuge in trivial, miniature realms and "odes on objects." Wang singles out Zhu Yizun as an example, asserting that Zhu hobbled his creative talents, "afraid to purchase peril with his writings."[35] I suppose that the Manchu literary inquisitions may have contributed to the constraints on Qing lyricists, though in comparison with the constraints imposed by generic convention they seem of secondary importance.

The role played by music, while an unresolved issue, was instrumental in limiting the achievements of Qing lyricists. It is a truism in Chinese literature that most flourishing poetic genres have been fertilized by popular songs and often by foreign music. Music from Serindia is supposed to have inspired the "music archive ballads" performed in the Western Han court. Songs from Kucha and elsewhere in Central Asia played a role in the gestation of the lyric. The twelfth-century Jin invasion brought the "medley" to maturity, while the Mongol conquest occasioned the rise of the "dramatic lyric."[36] But the Manchus brought no indigenous musical form with them, although they did produce a

Singde, for which we must be grateful. And, though Chinese lyricists derived inspiration from singing girls and may even have written lyrics with the strains of popular Kunshan tunes in their ears, it seems the seventeenth-century lyric was no longer wedded to a corpus of popular music. Instead, Qing lyricists composed "by the book"; thus, lyrical prosody suffered the same type of ossification that had robbed the Yuan dramatic lyric of its vitality.[37] The failure of Chinese lyricists to remarry lyrics and music was crucial to their inability to match the achievements of Soong versifiers.

Thus, I must concur with Chinese critics that even the best seventeenth-century lyrics remain poetry of the second rank.[38] But Zheng Qian's grade for seventeenth century lyricists, C on a scale from A+ to C-, is surely too harsh.[39] If we must treat lyricists like schoolchildren and award the best Soong lyrics an A+, then surely the best lyrics in this book deserve no lower than an A-!

A survey of Qing lyrics as a whole lies beyond my scope here. I do wish, however, to take issue with another cliché that distorts how we understand the development of Qing lyrics. Many critics argue that "elevating the form" *(zun ti)* was the key Qing contribution to the lyric genre and the factor accounting for its renaissance.[40] Actually, "elevating" the lyric had just the opposite effect. As the lyric betrayed its roots in courtesan's parlors and entertainment halls, it lost its vitality. This is borne out by the subsequent history of Qing lyrics. As divergent views about the genre hardened into the West Zhejiang and Changzhou factions, the *study and criticism* of lyrics flourished. While West Zhejiang critics worshiped the meticulous craft and formal perfection of southern Soong lyrics, the Changzhou critics delved deep to recover allegorical meanings from verse. Indeed, their determined efforts to uncover hidden significance in even the most innocuous lyric have retained their influence even in the twentieth century.[41] Yet the lyrics produced by their adherents are by no means easy to distinguish, and neither faction produced an outstanding lyricist.[42] For great poetry (as opposed to great criticism), China had to wait for the upheavals of the mid-nineteenth century. This suggests once again that political crises, not theoretical refinements, spurred Chinese literati to aesthetic creativity.

In conclusion, let us not underestimate the seventeenth-century lyric. Modern literary historians may relegate its remarkable resurgence to a mere footnote, remarking only how it demonstrates that genres do not so much "wear out" as gain or lose popularity according to vicissitudes of social and cultural change.[43] But if the seventeenth-century "elevation" of lyrics did not carry the genre to new heights, the poets in this book did produce much refined and beautiful verse. History, literary and otherwise, is full of injustices. Yet it would seem particularly unfair if critics could not find for the seventeenth-century lyric a slim chapter in the voluminous history of Chinese literature.

Notes

Chapter One. Introduction

1. For translations of *ci,* see Liu 1974:1 and Sun 1980:1.

2. Hucker 1961:3–4, 52.

3. During the 1620s, these officials were called the "East Wood" faction; for studies, see Hucker 1957 and the bibliography in Wakeman 1985.

4. Hucker 1957:156.

5. For examples, including one of the poets in this volume, Chen Zilong, see Peterson 1979:117–118.

6. See Wakeman 1985:2–4 and Peterson 1979:70.

7. See esp. Wakeman 1985:1–9.

8. See Chan 1982:224, 245 and Struve 1984:2.

9. See Wakeman 1985:227.

10. See esp. Chan 1982:52–63, 347.

11. Dennerline 1981:62–63.

12. See Struve 1984: chaps. 1, 2.

13. A good source on this period is Kessler 1976.

14. Wakeman 1985:55–56 and Sun 1973:7.

15. Wakeman 1985:643–644.

16. On Qian Qianyi, see Hummel 1943, 1:148–158. On Gu Yanwu, see Hummel 1943, 1:421–426. In dividing Chinese literati into "romantics," "stoics," and "martyrs," I am following Wakeman 1984.

17. This was true particularly for southern Chinese scholars; see Struve 1979:324 and Struve 1984.

18. On Manchu nativism in the 1660s, see Oxnam 1970.

19. Wakeman 1975:11–12.

20. See Kessler 1976:31–39.

21. Struve 1979:332; Peterson 1979:99–100.

22. Dennerline 1981:313.

23. Zheng 1961:165.

24. Li Mengyang's slogan has been widely quoted (e.g., Lynn 1975:232).

25. See Guo Shaoyu 1970:298–299, 323. I refer to Wang by his courtesy name, Yuanmei, because his given name, Shizhen, would confuse him with a seventeenth-century poet named Wang Shizhen, whom I will discuss below.

26. For favors conferred on You Tong, see He 1971:6 and Dolby 1976:116; for information on Chen, Zhu, and Nalan, see below.

27. Compare Aoki 1969:180.

28. Zheng 1961:167.

29. See Wakeman 1985:102, quoting a remark by Yoshikawa Kojiro.

30. HHL: preface, 2a; cf. Chu 1978:51.

31. CHCB, 12:4057; cf. 2:607.

32. For detailed knowledge, the reader is referred to Liu 1974, and Sun 1980. For information about Chinese poets and genres mentioned in this book, see esp. Liu and Lo 1975, Nienhauser 1986, and the appendices in Frankel 1976:212–217 and Sun 1980:210–212.

33. Compare Lin 1978:196–197.

34. See esp. Lin 1978:99–121.

35. See Liu 1974:3–4, Sun 1980:1–2, 8–9, and Wagner 1984, esp. ix–x.

36. For examples of romantic longing, see the selections in Fusek 1982. For examples of refined sentiment, see the lyrics of Feng Yansi translated in Bryant 1982.

37. Feng 1969, esp. 189–191; cf. Liu 1974:53–99 and Sun 1980:107–157.

38. See esp. Liu 1974:121–160 and Sun 1980:156–206.

39. Sun 1980:205; cf. Liu 1974:161–194.

40. See Lo 1971.

41. Liu 1973:140; Lin 1978:11–12.

Chapter Two. Chen Zilong

1. Quoted in Struve 1984:iii.

2. Quoted in Atwell 1975:12.

3. On the Ming archaists, see Lynn 1983:317–340. On the political roles of the study groups, see Atwell 1974:333–367.

4. The incident is discussed in Atwell 1975:39. Compare Wang Yun's account in CZYNP:1.11b, which mentions no fisticuffs.

5. With typical pride, Chen claimed to be "at the top" of the list; see CZYNP:2.7a.

6. CZYNP:2.10b–13b. The ramifications of this affair have been studied in Dennerline 1979:91–135.

7. Wakeman 1985:666. Note that, in CZYNP:2.31a, written during the sensitive years of the early Qing, Chen's role in the mutiny is minimized.

8. Quoted in CZYNP:3.10b.

9. It is unknown exactly where Chen died, and the accuracy of Wang Yun's account is in question (see Atwell 1975:177, n. 64). As Struve 1979:336 warns, family-sponsored histories of the time often "dramatized and embellished" the deaths of their loved ones. While I doubt that Chen's chronobiography engages in wholesale fabrication, it would be naive not to suspect that it enhances episodes portraying Chen in a heroic light and suppresses episodes placing Chen in an unfavorable light.

10. See Wang Yun's account in *Sanshi Kujie Zhuan* (appended to Chen's chronobiography), 22b. Compare Atwell 1975:55.

11. CZYNP:3.30a.

12. Ms. Liu's retort is quoted in Chen 1980, 1:89.

13. Luo's supposition is quoted in Chen 1980, 1:42–43.

14. For the evidence, see Chen 1980, esp. 1:235–296.

15. For selections from Ms. Liu's poetry, see Chen 1980:passim. I use the term *geisha* to suggest that high-class female entertainers usually formed liaisons with literary patrons but were not common prostitutes. *Geisha* has been used before in this context (e.g., in Hung 1952:55).

16. The common wisdom is that Qing lyrics were wholly divorced from music (see, e.g., Zheng 1961:163). So laments Qing critic Liu Tiren on the loss of Soong music and prosodic rules: "The beauty of ancient lyrics lay entirely in the realm of prosody; now men look upon lyrics as a mere matter of words" (CHCB, 2:628; cf. n. 10 above).

But it does not logically follow that, because Soong music was lost, lyrics lost all connection with music. Naturally, written proof of such a connection is hard to find. But consider this admission by Qing lyricist Mao Qiling (1623–1716): "When I was young and unconventional, I became known as a tunesmith; all the songstresses used to come to me for instruction. I used to sing my own lyrics" (CHCB, 2:573).

Qing lyricists also refer to the performance of lyrics a few times in their verses (e.g., HHL:22.2b, where Chen Weisong mentions the singing of a lyric set to the tune *Charms of Niannu;* and MCJC:22.3a, where Wu Weiye mentions a lyric sung to the tune *Quelling Windswept Waves*). The *ci* lyric and southern *qu* dramatic lyrics had always been close cousins (many Chinese literati practically equated them; see, e.g., the comment by Song Xiangfeng, quoted in Long 1980:3). We find indirect confirmation of their mingling in the consternation with which Qing literati saw *ci* and *qu* being confused and in the vehemence with which they warned poets not to bastardize the lyric with *qu* prosody and diction (see esp. CHCB, 3:849, 8:2527; and Wu

Mei 1964:142–143). Since most Chinese poetic genres have flourished as a result of stimuli from popular music (Charles Hartman [in Nienhauser 1986: 72] sees this as the underlying pattern for every major Chinese poetic genre), it would indeed be surprising had seventeenth-century lyricists not been inspired by dramatic lyrics from Kunshan and elsewhere.

17. On the fame of Shengze, see Chen 1980, 1:328.

18. See Miner 1968:16.

19. As Cyril Birch does (see Birch 1965, 2:131).

20. Compare Bryant 1982:99.

21. In lines 6–7, I have adopted variant readings from Zheng 1978, 2:82–83.

22. This is the assessment of Chen's friend Fang Yizhi, quoted in Peterson 1979:29. For a selection of Chen's "lofty, serious" verse, see Shen Deqian 1933, 2:84–88.

23. See Chen 1980, 1:241, 271, 303–304.

24. For example, He 1971:5.

25. Chu 1978:49.

26. Zheng 1961:III.

27. Compare Bryant 1982:13.

28. See Bryant 1982:6, 13, 16.

29. See Ye 1970:143 and RJCH:12.

30. For a discussion of Feng's character, see Bryant 1982:xx–xxii.

31. CHCB, II:3275–3276.

32. CHCB, 10:3601.

33. CHCB, 2:678–679; II:4021.

Chapter Three. Wu Weiye

1. Zhao Yi 1963:130; see Chen Xiangyao 1984:16.

2. See *Yishi*, 29.

3. Hummel 1943, 2:883; cf. Goodrich 1935:100–101, 209–210. Wu's poetic works remained popular throughout the Qing—see Nienhauser 1986:902.

4. See Hummel 1943, 2:883.

5. See the note to Wu's "Song of Yuanyuan" in *Qingshixuan*, 32.

6. Ma 1935:55; 22, 25.

7. Ibid., 43; 45.

8. Ibid., 45.

9. Sun 1973:4, 5–6.

10. Ma 1935:55.

11. Sun 1973:3–4.

12. For a masterful account of this phase in Wu's life, see Wakeman 1985: 937–942.

13. Wakeman 1985:935. Zhu Yizun is quoted in Sun 1973:8, n. 56. Compare Wu's chronobiographer, Gu Mei, quoted in Ma 1935:45, 56.

14. WSJL:12B.8a. According to legend, Liu An, the prince of Huainan, concocted a successful immortality formula and ascended to heaven. His cocks and mutts licked the leftover bowl of elixir and followed him to heaven. Here, Wu is, of course, implying that he should have died for the Ming instead of serving the Qing.

15. MCJC:21.6a, 22.6a.

16. *Yishi*, 15.

17. Ma 1935:66; Wakeman 1985:1076.

18. See Dennerline 1975:109–119.

19. Hummel 1943, 2:882.

20. Wakeman 1984:637. Wu is quoted in Wakeman 1985:1078.

21. See Sun 1973:10 and Nienhauser 1986:902.

22. "Tear-runneled cheeks" refer to the effects of puffyness and tear stains on makeup—cf. Li Yu's *Gazing on Jiangnan* in Bryant 1982:71.

23. Bryant 1982:67.

24. On "Cloud Blossom" as mica, see PSTC:5.7a. On "Cloud Blossom" as a courtesan, see the story of Pei Hang, quoted in YSCJ:260. On "Master Xiao," see PSTC:4.26b.

25. Note that *zhu* here does not mean *stay* (as rendered in Birch 1965, 2:133). It is a particle common in southern songs that gives the preceding verb a perfective aspect. For this insight, I am grateful to Kao Kung-yi of Stanford University.

26. *Tsin Shu*, 42.1198.2.

27. *Charms of Niannu* is translated in Liu 1974:136ff. *Joy of Eternal Union* is translated in Lo 1971:71ff.

28. Liu 1974:142.

29. *Shiji*, 28.0117.1.

30. Yu 1983:685.

31. Dennerline 1981:1, chap. 10. Jiading is now part of greater Shanghai.

32. Qian 1893:123.19a.

33. See Fukumoto 1962:12.

34. Ibid.

35. Compare Paul Kroll's translation in Liu and Lo 1975:196.

36. CJZJ:30.2a.

37. True both of Wu's *shi* (Fukumoto 1962:11) and of his *ci* (CHCB, 9:3172).

38. *Yishi*, 58.

39. Sun 1980:76.

40. See Liu and Lo 1975:267ff.
41. CHCB, II:4215.
42. Wang 1979:64.
43. CHCB, II:4225.

Chapter Four. Wang Fuzhi

1. On Wang's materialist skepticism, see Teng 1968:113. On his view of historical change, see Wakeman 1985:1086.

2. Because Wang's thought inspired later Hunan revolutionaries like Tan Sitong (1865–1898) and Mao Zedong, modern Chinese scholars have produced dozens of studies of Wang's philosophy. The best studies of Wang's philosophy in English are McMorran 1974:415–455 and Wakeman 1985:1086–1090.

3. The quotation is from Soothill 1976:271. On Liang Qichao, see CSXP: 95; cf. Hou 1982:8.

4. On Wang's historical writings and his historiographical views, see Teng 1968:111–123.

5. For discussions, see Aoki 1969:32–36 and Wong 1978:121–150.

6. I concur with the assessment given in Chen Xiangyao 1984:3, 124.

7. For a recent study, see Wu Zeyu, 458–472.

8. Zhang 1965:1.

9. Ibid., 3.

10. Ibid.

11. CSXP:6, 15.

12. Struve 1984:125.

13. Compare Struve 1980:57.

14. Zhang 1965:5.

15. CSXP:20.

16. Zhang 1965:15.

17. CSXP:39.

18. Zhang 1965:16.

19. On the reform society, see McMorran 1979:143.

20. McMorran 1979:142; ibid., 1974:413.

21. Quoted extensively (e.g., Zhang 1965:5). A *chi* is a bit shorter than the English foot.

22. The phrase is from Wang's widely quoted tomb epitaph (e.g., Wu Zeyu, 458).

23. *Shiji,* 6.0025.1.

24. See Schafer 1973:65.

25. Ibid., 38–42.
26. Ibid., 67–68.
27. Lin 1978:64–81.
28. Ibid., 11ff.
29. See Yan 1974:29b–32a.
30. On Taiyi, see the note in Zhang 1983:360.
31. Liu 1973:141.
32. Ibid., 144. On the "impersonality" of the lyric subject in Jiang's lyrics, see Lin 1978:11.
33. For example, CHCB, 12:4191.
34. Compare Wu Zeyu, 463.
35. On patriotism, compare Wu Zeyu, 458ff.
36. Quoted in McMorran 1979:138.
37. Quoted in *Qingci Jinquan*, 14.
38. Takata in the source notes refers to Takata 1981, *O Senzan [Wang Chuanshan] Shibunshu*, a Japanese critical anthology of Wang's verse.
39. This verse is discussed in Wu Zeyu, 461.
40. McMorran 1974:423.
41. Hawkes 1959:90.
42. For examples from Asian poetry, see Lee 1979:33.
43. Except for the italicized binomes, Wang quotes a couplet by Wang Wan of the Tang (translated in Liu 1982:14).
44. For the anecdotes behind these lines, see ZZYD: 45/17/83–84; 7/3/8–10.
45. CHCB, 11:4191.
46. For a study of Wang Yisun's Soong loyalism and his allegorical "odes on objects," see Ye 1980.
47. Ge Zai, quoted in Zheng 1978:206; Yan 1974:90a; *Qingci Jinquan*, 16.
48. Ibid.
49. Wu Zeyu, 460, 471.
50. Yan 1974:92a; QSC, 5:3355. Ye 1980:62 argues that Yisun's lyric expresses sorrow for the fate of Soong empresses and consorts after the dynasty's fall. Wang Fuzhi undoubtedly read the lyric this way.
51. Ye 1980:83–84. Compare Zheng 1972:261, who notes the accusation that Wang Yisun "has [good] lines, but no [good] lyrics."
52. For an example, see Wang Fuzhi's *Riverful of Red* in GZCJ:9b–10a, which is compared to Su's lyrics in Wu Zeyu, 460.
53. For an analysis of the key role that allegory played in Changzhou criticism, see Ye 1978:151–188.
54. Quoted in Lin 1979:367.

Chapter Five. Chen Weisong

1. MB:706; Chu 1978:14.

2. Chu 1978:19.

3. Kessler 1976:154.

4. For the Jiangnan Tax Arrears Case, see Oxnam 1970:102–108 and Kessler 1976:33–39. For the Ming History Case, see Oxnam 1970:108–112 and Kessler 1976:31–32.

5. See Qian 1962:474.

6. Mao was one of the "Four Lords" of the late Ming (Qinian's father was another) and a leading exponent of late Ming erotic aestheticism—see Wakeman 1985:756, n. 114.

7. Chu 1978:21–23.

8. Ibid., 23–24.

9. Huang 1983:247.

10. Eighty percent of the successful candidates were southerners—see Kessler 1976:161. More than half had already served the Manchus, but no Ming officials passed—see Peterson 1969:240.

11. Qian 1893:45.19b.

12. Ibid., 45.20a.

13. CHCB, 7:2354; 10:3534.

14. For a translation, see Chu 1978:79–80.

15. Qian 1893:45.20b.

16. Ibid., 45.21a.

17. *Nan Shi,* 55.2674.1.

18. See Schafer 1972:983–984.

19. See Mather 1976:128.

20. Qinian's topical verse is discussed in Qian 1962:475–477.

21. Chu 1978:86.

22. Ibid.

23. Chen 1983, 1:7; CHCB, 9:3714.

24. Qian 1962:481.

25. Ibid., 482.

26. CHCB, 12:4277.

27. Struve 1979:324.

28. See the discussion in Chu 1978:70.

29. Chu 1978:72.

30. See CHCB, 10:3367. For Zhu's lyric describing Qinian as a black bull, see PSTC:2.10b.

31. TSSJY:296.

32. Quoted from Ye 1973:166. In her discussion, Ye observes that Wu bor-

rowed his "sour wind" from Li He's line, "A sour wind from the eastern pass impales the eyes."

33. Translation from Liu 1974:139.

34. TSSJY:657.

35. CHCB, 10:3294.

36. Qian 1962:475.

37. Translated in Lo 1986:101–102.

38. He 1971:36.

39. Ibid., 38.

40. See Lo 1971:68–69.

41. Liu 1974:154.

42. Lo 1971:14.

43. Liu 1974:139–140; Lo 1971:71.

44. Yoshikawa 1968:152.

45. In the process, Qinian exerted a strong influence on later "allegorical" schools of lyrical criticism—see Qian 1962:483.

46. Chu 1978, esp. 52–53, 109–110.

47. Zheng 1972:263.

48. Here, I disagree with Chen 1983, 1:327.

Chapter Six. Zhu Yizun

1. Lynn 1983:162.

2. Hummel 1943, 1:184.

3. Zhang 1978:78 and Yoshikawa 1968:151–152.

4. SKTY:3722.

5. Yang, 6a.

6. Wakeman 1985:651–652.

7. Yang, 7a–8b.

8. Hummel 1943, 1:182.

9. Yang, 9a. Compare Wakeman 1985:939.

10. PSTJ:36.13a. Compare Gao 1984:214.

11. Peterson 1969:232.

12. See Yang, 20a.

13. For a description of the emperor's lively intellectual curiosity, see Kessler 1976:141–142.

14. Yang, 29a.

15. Kessler 1976:163.

16. Yang, 38a.

17. Ibid., 42a.

18. PSTJ:7.6a–9a.
19. Quoted in Gao 1984:215–216.
20. Zhang 1978:70–71.
21. PSTC:1.30b. Compare CHCB, 6:2055 and 10:3312–3313.
22. CHCB, 4:1469.
23. PSTJ:36.5a; cf. Gao 1984:214–215.
24. Yang, 6b.
25. Hummel 1943, 1:184.
26. Huang 1983. Yang, 26b explicitly denies the anecdote.
27. Hummel 1943, 1:183.
28. Qian 1893:45.16a.
29. For example, PSTJ:40.6b; Aoki 1969:189; Lin 1979, 1:133.
30. See, for example, Aoki 1969:81 and Yoshikawa 1968:151–152.
31. Gao 1984:208–213; Lin 1979, 1:15; CHCB, 8:2596; Zhang 1978:78; Gao 1984:216–217.
32. Compare Frankel 1976:149.
33. See Frankel 1974:345–346.
34. Especially Chen 1983, 1:291; Chen was not normally an enthusiast of Zhu's lyrics.
35. Kellogg and Scholes 1966:268.
36. ZZYD: II/1/4.
37. Liu 1974:148.
38. See Sun 1980:37.
39. Sikong Tu 1966:42.
40. For example, CHCB, 7:2556, 10:3423, and 11:4034; Zhang 1978:78.
41. For example, Wu 1964:164.
42. CHCB, 7:2420.
43. Yoshikawa 1968:151.
44. CHCB, 5:1515.
45. Wang 1979:74, 79.
46. This is an ode on "Withered Lotuses." Li Shangyin's original line ran, "Leaving behind withered lotuses to listen for sounds of rain."
47. This is from an ode on "Cicadas." Jiang Kui, in his ode on crickets, wrote:

> Laugh: at [bug-catching] boys and girls of the world
> Who call for lamps by the fence.

Compare Lin 1978:179.
48. Six Dynasties politician Xie An's dream of a white cock presaged the hour of his demise. Vermilion Bird Bridge at sunset evokes the vanished glory of the Six Dynasties—see tune 28 above.

49. Liu 1974:8, 159.
50. Quoted in CHCB, 12:4230; cf. 10:3505.
51. For example, CHCB, 9:3165.
52. CHCB, 12:4096.
53. PSTJ:40.5b.
54. Widely quoted (e.g., in Yoshikawa 1968:145).
55. Yoshikawa 1968:151. For a few exceptions, see He 1971:50.
56. Here, *spare* suggests a style that is flexible and not overstuffed. Sun Kang-i has translated the term as *pure and visionary*—see Nienhauser 1986: 230–231. *Long Halt Lament* is compared with Zhang's lyrics in Chen 1983, 1:291. For other examples of Zhang's influence on Zhu, see Zhang 1978:74 and He 1971:50–51.
57. See Su 1979:247.
58. Chen 1983, 1:291.
59. Yoshikawa 1968:151.
60. CHCB, 7:2380.
61. These phrases are applied to Shi in Zheng 1978:203. They are applied to Zhu in He 1971:48 and Zheng 1978:74.
62. For other examples from Zhu's work, see Yoshikawa 1968:149 and Zhang 1978:73–74.
63. QSC, 4:2326.
64. CHCB, 8:2549.
65. That is, the moon.
66. QSC, 4:2342.
67. PSTJ:40.1b–2a. Most Chinese literati interpreted the *Songs of Chu* and the *Capitol Odes (ya)* from the *Book of Odes* allegorically.
68. Yoshikawa 1968:151.
69. For example, Gao 1984:216–217; Yoshikawa 1968:151.

Chapter Seven. Nalan Singde

1. RJCH:36.
2. His oeuvre preserves a lyric that Singde wrote on Primal Night, 1664, at the age of nine; see YSCJ:355.
3. Huang 1983:203.
4. Ibid., 209–211.
5. See the assessment by Liang Qiqiao quoted in YSCJ:60.
6. See William Schultz' note [in Nienhauser 1986:634].
7. Hummel 1943, 2:662.
8. Ibid.

9. Quoted in YSCJ:314.

10. See Hummel 1943, 2:663 and Huang 1983:214–215. For a lyric expressing Singde's determination to help Wu Zhaoqian, see YSCJ:485.

11. Ruan Kuisheng, quoted in YSCJ:56.

12. Nienhauser 1986:634.

13. The line quoted reworks Du Fu's famous conclusion to the "Song of the Ancient Cypress": "Since antiquity, hard for great timber/talent to find a use" (DSYD 109/10/24).

14. Huang 1983:142.

15. A point made by Schultz [in Nienhauser 1986:635].

16. Quoted in Huang 1983:3.

17. Kessler 1976: chap. 5; Hummel 1943, 2:577.

18. Hummel 1943, 2:311.

19. Huang 1983:56.

20. For example, Hu 1935:17–18.

21. RJCH:35.

22. *Nan Shi*, 17.2591.1.

23. See Huang 1983:344.

24. See Liu 1969:139.

25. See the note in Liu and Lo 1975:486.

26. Hu 1935:15.

27. Min 1969:173b, n. 1.

28. Compare Mather 1976:387.

29. Huang 1983:188.

30. Translation from Liu 1974:43.

31. Compare Liu 1962:44.

32. See Zheng 1978, 2: app. 9.

33. YSCJ contains 344 lyrics, Hu Yunyi's edition only 311. Doubts have been raised about the authenticity of a few lyrics; see, for example, CHCB, 10:3425–3426.

34. Hu 1935:17.

35. Schultz [in Nienhauser 1986:635].

36. Hu 1935:5, Min 1969:256b, and Li Xu in his preface to YSCJ.

37. Hu 1935:3–4.

38. Ibid., 17.

39. Huang 1983:131.

40. Ibid., 31.

41. Hu 1935:13.

42. See Sun 1980:40, 49.

43. For lyrics with a pronounced dramatic bent, see YSCJ:107, 317. Compare Huang 1983:179.

44. For example, Hu 1935:17–18.

45. Quoted in Sun 1980:72.

46. These two lines allude to the opening and closing of Li's famous "Ornamented Zither":

> The ornamented zither, for no reason, has fifty strings;
> Each string, each bridge, recalls a burgeoning year. . . .
> This feeling might have become a memory to be cherished,
> But for that, even then, it already seemed an illusion.

See Liu's translation in Liu and Lo 1975:240.

47. A note to YSCJ:209 gives the source in Li Shangyin's work. We encountered the story of Han Ping and his wife above. For a discussion of this allusion's importance in Singde's poetry, see Huang 1983:56–57.

48. Liu 1969:214.

49. Ibid., 212.

50. See Zheng 1984, esp. 72–75. As Zheng notes, it was Singde's friend, Yan Shengsun, who wrote a preface for Wang Cihui's collection.

51. Wang Cihui's ode on "The Moon" includes the line, "She furtively reveals her comely beauty by the doorknocker."

52. A note to YSCJ:181 provides the former line's source in a Wei Zhuang lyric. The latter line recalls Yan Jidao's celebrated conclusion to *Immortal Approaching the River:*

> The full moon from back then remains;
> Once it shone on Colored Cloud returning. (QSC, 1:222)

53. "Mlle. Xie" is a conventional term for a desirable woman. The note in YSCJ quotes a line from Wei Zhuang's lyrics, but Singde's readers would have recognized an allusion to Yan Jidao's famous couplet:

> My dreaming soul, long used to having no constraints,
> Traipsed again over willow flowers on a visit to Xie's Bridge. (QSC, 1:227)

Yan's couplet moved even straitlaced Cheng Yi, who disapproved of poetry, to exclaim: "Demonic words!" (quoted in CHCB, 3:1034).

54. Here, Singde interweaves references to two lyrics Yan Jidao wrote to the tune *Picking Silkworms*—see QSC, 1:252.

55. CHCB, 11:3429, 4023; Chen 1983, 1:261. For examples from Singde's poetry, see esp. YSCJ:86–87, 94, 100, 358, 399.

56. See Huang 1983:176–177. On the importance of "native sensibility" and related concepts in the seventeenth century, see Liu 1975:80–83.

57. Sun 1980:44.

58. Ibid., 59.

59. Ibid., 60.

60. The two rulers were Li Yu and his father, Li Jing. Chen Weisong's

comment is quoted in Zheng 1978, 2: app. 8. For other, similar judgments, see YSCJ:50.

61. The "plain sketch" is discussed as a characteristic of Li Yu's later lyrics in Shao 1973:1; Sun 1980:90; ibid., 70–71.

62. Ye 1970:118, explicating a comment by Wang Guowei in RJCH:11–12.

63. Zheng 1961:116.

64. QSC, 1:255.

65. QSC, 1:224.

66. Feng Xu, quoted in Zheng 1978, 1:188.

67. Zheng 1961:116–117. Lin 1975:33–40 lists more than seventy examples from Yan's lyrics.

68. Quoted in Huang 1983:36. For a similar assessment, see CHCB, 11: 4023.

69. RJCH:36.

70. Ibid.

71. Hu 1935:18.

72. Chen 1983, 1:45, 259. Compare Lin 1975:92.

73. CHCB, 12:4215; quoted approvingly in Zheng 1978, 2: app. 9 and Wang 1973:133.

Chapter Eight. Conclusion

1. These terms are quoted from Liu 1974:194 and RJCH, esp. 26–28, respectively.

2. Quoted in Huang 1983:174–175.

3. Wakeman 1985:422–423.

4. CHCB, 3:1118.

5. *Luzhai Ji*, 2; Long 1962:5.

6. Kuang Zhouyi, quoted in Lin 1979, 3:368.

7. See the explication of Wang Shizhen's key term *shenyun* as "spirit and tone" in Liu 1975:44. Lynn 1970:209–211 points out that Wang's modern-style verse accords with his theories. For appraisals of Wang's lyrics that feature the term *shenyun* or the synonymous *fengyun*, see Wu 1964:157 and He 1971:9.

8. So argues Xie Zhangting in CHCB, 10:3601.

9. *Yanpo Ji*, 1.8.

10. Lin 1978:120.

11. TSSJY, 2:790. Compare Kao and Mei 1971:101.

12. TSSJY, 2:846.

13. Kao and Mei 1978:309.

14. Kao and Mei 1976, esp. 134 observe that Wang's quatrains often end with a reference to the past to deepen their "lingering overtones."

15. *Yanpo Ji,* 2.1.
16. See Wang 1964:117.
17. For example, Chen 1983, 1:257 and Wu 1964:158.
18. See Long 1962:2 and CHCB, 3:1486.
19. This verdict is shared by Zhu Yizun, quoted in CHCB, 7:1827. Compare Wu 1964:158.
20. *Kexue Ci,* 1.20b.
21. See LDSX, 2:618.
22. Translation from Liu 1962:52.
23. DSYD 47/3/15–16.
24. *Qingci Jinquan,* 25.
25. Compare Liu and Lo 1975:178.
26. *Tanzhi Ci,* 2.20b–21a. For examples of the high praise awarded these lyrics, see CHCB, 10:3423; Wu 1964:160.
27. Chen 1983, 1:274. Compare CHCB, 6:1827.
28. See Huang 1983:241.
29. *Tanzhi Ci,* 2.14a.
30. Su Shi translated in Liu 1974:139. Xin Qiji in Deng 1962:37.
31. Lin 1979, 1:2.
32. See Lee 1979, who identifies this as a basic trait common to East Asian classical poetry.
33. See Lynn 1983:162ff.
34. Quoted in Aoki 1969:183.
35. Wang 1979:67, 73.
36. See Dolby 1976:35ff.
37. Ibid., 58.
38. Compare Hu 1935:1; Chen 1983, 2:359.
39. Zheng 1961:162.
40. For example, Ye Gongchuo, quoted in Lin 1979, 3:490. Compare Chu 1978, esp. 49–52.
41. See Ye 1978.
42. Hu 1949: pt. 3:2. For this verdict, see He 1971:6; Chen 1983, 2:359; Lin 1979, 1:134–139.
43. This point was argued eloquently in Levenson 1957:338–339. Contrast Hartman [in Nienhauser 1986:73], who in tracing the lyric's evolution from popular poetry to "fossilized allegory" seems to attribute an inherent lifespan to the genre, as if art itself, rather than artists, determines when a genre has been exhausted.

Bibliography

Works in Chinese and Japanese

Aoki Masaru. 1969. *Qingdai Wenxue Pinglun Shi*. Translated by Chen Shunu. Taibei.

Cao Zhenji. *Kexue Ci*. SBBY.

Chen Tingzhuo. 1983. *Baiyuzhai Cihua Zuben Jiaozhu*. 2 vols. Jinan.

Chen Weisong. *Chen Jialing Wenji*. SBCK.

———. *Huhailou Ciji*. SBBY.

Chen Xiangyao, ed. 1984. *Qing Shixuan*. Beijing.

Chen Yinque. 1980. *Liu Rushi Biezhuan*. 3 vols. Shanghai.

Chen Yuyi. *Jianzhai Shiji*. SBBY.

Chen Zilong. *Chen Zhongyu Quanji*. Preface dated 1803.

———. *Xiangzhen Ci*. CZYQJ, vol. 20.

Cixue Yanjiu Lunwenji. 1983. Beijing.

Deng Guangming. 1962. *Xin Jiaxuan Ci Biannian Jianzhu*. Beijing.

Ding Ying, ed. 1979. *Lidai Shixuan*. 3 vols. Hong Kong.

Fang Xuanling. *Jinshu*. Kaiming ed.

Feng Qiyong. 1969. "Lun Bei Song Qianqi Liangzhong Butongde Cifeng." In *Tang Song Ci Yanjiu Lunwenji*. Beijing.

Fukumoto Masakazu. 1962. *Go Igyo*. Chugoku Shijin Senshu, ser. 2, no. 12. Tokyo.

Gao Buying, comp. 1978. *Tang Song Shi Juyao*. 2 vols. Hong Kong.

Gao Jianzhong. 1984. "Zhu Yizun Shilun Zhitan." In *Gudai Wenxue Lilun Yanjiu*, edited by Xu Zhongyu, 208–219. Shanghai.

Gu Zhenguan. *Tanzhi Ci*. SBBY.

Guo Shaoyu. 1970. *Zhongguo Wenxue Pipingshi*. Hong Kong.

He Guangzhong. 1971. *Lun Qingci*. Taibei.

Hou Wailu. 1982. *Chuanshan Xue'an*. Changsha.

Hu Yunyi, ed. 1935. *Yinshui Ciji.* Shanghai.

———. 1949. *Cixue Xiao Congshu.* 2 vols. Shanghai.

Huang Tianji. 1983. *Nalan Singde he Tade Ci.* Guangdong.

Hung Yeh. 1966a. *A Concordance to the Poetry of Du Fu.* HYSIS.

———. 1966b. *A Concordance to Zhuangzi.* HYSIS.

Ji Yun et al., eds. 1931. *Siku Quanshu Zongmu Tiyao.* 8 vols. Shanghai.

Li Wen. 1963. *Luzhai Ji.* Compiled by Chen Naiqian. Vol. 7 in Qing Mingjia Cixuan, 10 vols. Hong Kong.

Li Yanshou. 1935. *Nanshi.* Kaiming ed. Shanghai.

Lin Meiyi. 1979. "Wanqing Cixue Yanjiu." 3 vols. Ph.D. diss., Taiwan University.

Lin Mingde. 1975. *Yan Jidao ji qi Ci.* Taibei.

Long Muxun, comp. 1962. *Jin Sanbainian Mingjia Cixuan.* Shanghai.

———. 1980. *Ci Qu Gailun.* Shanghai.

Ma Daoyuan. 1935. *Wu Meicun Nianpu.* Shanghai.

Min Zongshu. 1969. *Yinshui Ci Bujian.* Taibei.

Nalan Singde. 1959. *Yinshui Ci Jian.* Compiled by Li Xu. Taibei.

Qian Yiji, comp. 1893. *Beizhuan Ji.* Jiangsu.

Qian Zhonglian. 1962. "Lun Chen Weisong de Huhailou Ci." In *Cixue Yanjiu Lunwenji,* 473–483.

Shen Deqian, comp. 1933. *Mingshi Biecai.* 2 vols. Shanghai.

Sikong Tu. 1966. *Sikong Tu Shipin Zhushi ji Yiben,* edited by Zu Baoquan. Hong Kong.

Sima Qian. *Shiji.* Kaiming ed.

Su Wenting. 1979. *Songdai Yimin Wenxue Yanjiu.* Taibei.

Sun Kekuan. 1974. "Wu Meicun Beixing Qianhou Shi." *Guoli Zhongyang Tushuguan Guankan.* 7, no. 1 (March): 3–13.

Takata Atsushi. 1981. *O Senzan [Wang Chuanshan] Shibunshu.* Tokyo.

Tang Guizhang, ed. 1965. *Quan Songci.* 5 vols. Shanghai.

———, ed. 1967. *Cihua Congbian.* 12 vols. Taibei.

Wang Fuzhi. 1961. *Chuci Tongshi.* Hong Kong.

———. *Guzhuo Chuji.* SBCK ed., vol. 60.

———. *Guzhuo Erji.* SBCK ed., vol. 61.

———. *Wang Chuanshan Shiwen.* Beijing.

———. *Xiao Xiang Yuanci.* SBCK.

Wang Jiyou. 1979. *Zhiyuan Cihua.* Hong Kong.

Wang Shizhen. *Yanpo Ji.* CSJC.

Wang Xiaoyu. 1975. *Wang Chuanshan Xuepu.* Taibei.

Wang Xiyuan. 1973. *Lidai Cihua Xulu.* Taibei.

Wang Yiqing et al., eds. 1964. *Qinding Cipu.* Taibei. Reprint of 1715 ed.

Wang Yun, comp. *Chen Zhongyu Nianpu.* CZYQJ, vol. 1.

Wang Zhiyuan. 1964. *Lidai Ciqu Pingxuan.* Taibei.

Wang Zhong. 1965. *Qing Ci Quan.* Taibei.

Wu Mei. 1964. *Cixue Tonglun.* Taibei.

Wu Meicun Yishi [attributed to "Bailong Shanren"]. Shanghai, n.d.

Wu Weiye. *Meicun Jiacang Gao.* SBCK.

———. *Wushi Jilan.* Annotated by Jin Rongfan. SBBY.

Wu Zeyu. "Jiangzhai Ci Lunlue." In *Cixue Yanjiu Lunwenji,* 458–472.

Yan Tianyou. 1974. *Nan Song Jiang Wu Cipai Yanjiu.* Taibei.

Yang Qian. *Zhu Zhucha Xiansheng Nianpu.* PSTJ, vol. 1.

Ye Jiaying. 1970. *Jialing Tanci.* Taibei.

Yoshikawa Kojiro. 1968. "Jutsu *Boshotei Shi,*" 144–152. In vol. 16 of Yoshikawa Kojiro Zenshu, 19 vol. Tokyo.

Yu Pingbo. 1983. *Lun Shiciqu Zazhu.* Shanghai.

Zhang Shaozhen. 1978. "Qingdai Zhejiang Cipai Yanjiu." M.A. thesis, Dongwu University.

Zhang Xitang. 1965. *Wang Chuanshan Xuepu.* Taibei.

Zhang Zhang, ed. 1983. *Lidai Cicui.* Henan.

Zhao Yi. 1963. *Oubei Shihua.* Beijing.

Zheng Qian. 1961. *Cong Shi Dao Qu.* Taibei.

———. 1972. *Jingwu Congbian.* 2 vols. Taibei.

———, comp. 1978. *Cixuan.* 2 vols. Taibei.

Zheng Qingmao, comp. 1984. *Wang Cihui Shiji.* Taibei.

Zhu Yizun. Preface dated 1814. *Pushuting Ci.* Annotated by Li Fusun.

———. *Pushuting Quanji.* SBBY.

Works in English

Atwell, William S. 1974. "From Education to Politics: The *Fushe.*" In *The Unfolding of Neo-Confucianism,* 333–367. *See* deBary 1975.

———. 1975. "Chen Tzu-lung: 1608–1647." Ph.D. diss., Princeton University.

Birch, Cyril, ed. 1965. *An Anthology of Chinese Literature.* 2 vols. New York.

———, ed. 1973. *Studies in Chinese Literary Genres.* Berkeley, Calif.

Bryant, Daniel. 1979. "The Rhyming Categories of Tenth Century Chinese Poetry," *Monumenta Serica* 34:319–347.

———. 1982. *Lyric Poets of the Southern T'ang.* Vancouver.

Chan, Albert. 1982. *The Glory and Fall of the Ming Dynasty.* Norman, Okla.

Chu, Madeline. 1978. *Ch'en Weisong, the Tz'u Poet.* Ph.D. diss., University of Arizona.

deBary, William T., ed. 1975. *The Unfolding of Neo-Confucianism.* New York.

Dennerline, Jerry. 1975. "Fiscal Reform and Local Control: the Gentry Bureaucratic Alliance Survives the Conquest." In *Conflict and Control in Late Imperial China*, 86–120. *See* Wakeman and Grant 1975.

———. 1979. "Hsu Tu and the Lesson of Nanking." In *From Ming to Ch'ing*, 91–135. *See* Spence 1979.

———. 1981. *The Chia-ting Loyalists: Confucian Leadership and Social Control in Seventeenth Century China*. New Haven, Conn.

Dolby, William. 1976. *A History of Chinese Theater*. New York.

Fairbank, John K., ed. 1957. *Chinese Thought and Institutions*. Chicago.

Frankel, Hans. 1976. *The Flowering Plum and the Palace Lady*. New Haven.

———. 1983. "The Contemplation of the Past in T'ang Poetry." In *Perspectives on the T'ang*, 345–365. *See* Wright and Twitchett 1983.

Fusek, Lois. 1982. *Among the Flowers*. New York.

Goodrich, L. Carrington. 1935. *The Literary Inquisition of Ch'ien-lung*. Baltimore.

Goodrich, L. Carrington, and Fang Chao-ying, eds. 1970. *Dictionary of Ming Biographies*. 2 vols. New York.

Hawkes, David. 1959. *Ch'u Tz'u: Songs of the South*. Boston.

Hucker, Charles. 1957. "The Tung-lin Movement of the Late Ming Period." In *Chinese Thought and Institutions*, 133–162. *See* Fairbank 1957.

———. 1961. *The Traditional Chinese State in Ming Times*. Tempe, Ariz.

Hummel, Arthur, ed. 1943. *Eminent Chinese of the Ch'ing Period*. 3 vols. Washington, D.C.

Hung, William. 1952. *Tu Fu: China's Greatest Poet*. New York.

Kao Yu-kung and Mei Tsu-lin. 1971. "Syntax, Diction and Imagery in T'ang Poetry." *Harvard Journal of Asiatic Studies* 31 (1971): 49–136.

———. 1976. "Ending Lines in Wang Shih-chen's *ch'i-chueh:* Convention and Creativity in the Ch'ing." In *Artists and Traditions*, 131–144. *See* Murck 1976.

———. 1978. "Meaning, Metaphor and Allusion in T'ang Poetry." *Harvard Journal of Asiatic Studies* 38 (1978): 281–356.

Kellogg, Robert, and Robert Scholes. 1966. *The Nature of Narrative*. New York.

Kessler, Lawrence. 1976. *Kang-hsi and the Consolidation of Ch'ing Rule, 1661–1684*. Chicago.

Lee, Peter H. 1979. *Celebration of Continuity*. Cambridge, Mass.

Levenson, Joseph. 1957. "The Amateur Ideal in Ming and Early Ch'ing Society." In *Chinese Thought and Institutions*, 320–341. *See* Fairbank 1957.

Lin Shuenfu. 1978. *The Transformation of the Chinese Lyrical Tradition: Chiang K'uei and Southern Sung Tz'u Poetry*. Princeton, N.J.

Liu I-ch'ing. 1976. *A New Account of Tales from the World*. Translated by Richard Mather. Minneapolis.

Liu, James J. Y. 1962. *The Art of Chinese Poetry*. Chicago.

———. 1969. *The Poetry of Li Shang-yin*. Chicago.

———. 1973. "Some Literary Qualities of the Lyric (Tz'u)." In *Studies in Chinese Literary Genres*, 133–153. See Birch 1973.

———. 1974. *Major Lyricists of the Northern Sung*. Princeton, N.J.

———. 1975. *Chinese Theories of Literature*. Chicago.

———. 1981. *The Interlingual Critic*. Bloomington, Ind.

———. 1982. Review of Stephen Owen's *The Golden Age of Chinese Poetry*. *Chinese Literature* 4, no. 1 (January): 94–104.

Liu Wu-chi and Irving Yucheng Lo, eds. 1975. *Sunflower Splendor*. New York.

Lo, Irving. 1971. *Hsin Ch'i-chi*. New York.

Lo, Irving, and William Schultz, eds. 1986. *Waiting for the Unicorn*. Bloomington, Ind.

Lynn, Richard. 1970. "Tradition and Synthesis: Wang Shih-chen as Poet and Critic." Ph.D. diss., Stanford University.

———. 1975. "Orthodoxy and Enlightenment: Wang Shih-chen's Theory of Poetry and Its Antecedents." In *The Unfolding of Neo-Confucianism*, 217–269. See deBary 1975.

———. 1983. "The Talent Learning Polarity in Chinese Poetics." *Chinese Literature* 5, no. 2 (1983): 157–184.

McMorran, Ian. 1975. "Wang Fu-chih and the Neo-Confucian Tradition." In *The Unfolding of Neo-Confucianism*, 413–455. See deBary 1975.

———. 1979. "The Patriot and the Partisans: Wang Fu-chih's Involvement in the Politics of the Yung-li Court." In *From Ming to Ch'ing*, 135–166. See Spence 1979.

Miner, Earl. 1968. *An Introduction to Japanese Court Poetry*. Stanford, Calif.

Murck, Christian, ed. 1976. *Artists and Traditions*. Princeton, N.J.

Nienhauser, William, ed. 1986. *The Indiana Companion to Traditional Chinese Literature*. Bloomington, Ind.

Oxnam, Robert. 1970. *Ruling from Horseback: Manchu Politics in the Oboi Regency, 1661–1669*. Chicago.

Peterson, Willard. 1969 "The Life of Ku Yen-wu (Part II)." *Harvard Journal of Asiatic Studies* 29 (1969): 201–246.

———. 1979. *Bitter Gourd: Fang Yi-chih and the Impetus for Intellectual Change*. New Haven, Conn.

Rickett, Adele A., ed. 1978. *Chinese Approaches to Literature from Confucius to Liang Ch'i-ch'ao*. Princeton, N.J.

Schafer, Edward. 1972. "Two Late T'ang Poems on Music." *Literature East and West* 16, no. 3 (1972): 979–996.

———. 1973. *The Divine Woman*. Berkeley, Calif.

Shao, Paul. 1973. "The Art of Depiction and the Lyrics of Li Yu." M.A. thesis, University of California at Berkeley.

Soothill, William, and Lewis Hodous. 1976. *A Dictionary of Chinese Buddhist Terms.* Taibei.

Spence, Jonathan, ed. 1979. *From Ming to Ch'ing.* New Haven, Conn.

Struve, Lynn. 1979. "Ambivalence and Action: Some Frustrated Scholars of the Kang-hsi Period." In *From Ming to Ch'ing,* 323–365. *See* Spence 1979.

————. 1980. "History and the *Peach Blossom Fan.*" *Chinese Literature* 2, no. 1:55–72.

————. 1984. *The Southern Ming.* New Haven, Conn.

Sun Chang Kang-i. 1980. *The Evolution of Chinese Tz'u Poetry, from Late T'ang to Northern Sung.* Princeton, N.J.

Teng Ssu-yu. 1968. "Wang Fu-chih's Views on History and Historical Writing." *Journal of Asian Studies* 28, no. 1 (November): 111–123.

Wakeman, Fred. 1984. "Romantics, Stoics, and Martyrs in Seventeenth Century China. *Journal of Asian Studies* 43, no. 4 (August): 631–665.

————. 1985. *The Great Enterprise.* 2 vols. Berkeley, Calif.

Wakeman, Fred, and Carolyn Grant, eds. 1975. *Conflict and Control in Late Imperial China.* Berkeley, Calif.

Wang Guowei. 1970. *Poetic Remarks in the Human World.* Translated by T'u Ching-i. Taibei.

Wong Siukit. 1978. "Ch'ing and Ching in the Critical Writings of Wang Fu-chih." In *Chinese Approaches to Literature from Confucius to Liang Ch'i-ch'ao,* 121–150. *See* Rickett 1978.

Wright, Arthur, and Denis Twitchett, eds. 1983. *Perspectives on the T'ang.* New Haven, Conn.

Ye Jiaying. 1978. "The Ch'ang-chou School of Tz'u Criticism." In *Chinese Approaches to Literature from Confucius to Liang Ch'i-chao.* 151–188. *See* Rickett 1978.

————. 1980. "On Wang Yi-sun and his Yung-wu Tz'u." *Harvard Journal of Asiatic Studies* 40, no. 1 (June): 55–91.

Chinese Texts

陳子龍

1 **點絳脣**　　春日風雨有感

滿眼韶華　　　　　夢裏相思
東風慣是吹紅去。　故國王孫路。
幾番烟霧。　　　　春無主。
只有花難護。　　　杜鵑啼處。
　　　　　　　　　淚染胭脂雨。

2 **畫堂春**　　雨中杏花

輕陰池館水平橋。　憶昔青門堤外
一番弄雨花梢。　　粉香零亂朝朝。
微寒著處不勝嬌。　玉顏寂寞淡紅飄。
此際魂消。　　　　無那今宵。

3 **山花子**　　春恨

楊柳迷離曉霧中。　蝶化綵衣金縷盡。
杏花零落五更鐘。　蟲銜畫粉玉樓空。
寂寂景陽宮外月　　惟有無情雙燕子
照殘紅。　　　　　舞東風。

179

4　江城子　　病起春盡

一簾病枕五更鐘。
曉雲空。
捲殘紅。
無情春色去矣,
幾時逢。
添我千行清淚也
留不住
苦恩恩。

楚宮吳苑草茸茸。
戀芳叢。
繞遊蜂。
料得來年相見,
畫屏中。
人自傷心花自笑
憑燕子
罵東風。

5　虞美人　　有感

夭桃紅杏春將半。
總被東風換。
王孫芳草路微茫。
只有青山依舊對斜陽。

綺羅如在無人到。
明月空相照。
夢中樓閣水湛湛。
撒下一天星露滿江南。

6　蝶戀花　　春日

雨外黃昏花外曉。
催得流年
有恨何時了。
燕子又來春漸老。
亂紅相對愁眉掃。

午夢闌珊歸路杳。
醒後思量
躑徧閒庭草。
幾度春風人意惱。
深深院落芳心小。

吳偉業

7　浣溪沙　　閨情

斷頰微紅眼半醒。
背人驀地下階行。
摘花高處賭身輕。

細撥薰鑪香繚繞。
嬾塗吟紙墨敧傾。
慣猜閒事為聰明。

8　臨江仙　　逢舊

落拓江湖常載酒
十年重見雲英。
依然綽約掌中輕。
燈前縱一笑
偷解石羅裙。

薄倖蕭郎憔悴甚
此生終負卿卿。
姑蘇城上月黃昏。
綠窗人去住
紅粉淚縱橫。

9　滿江紅　　蒜山懷古

沽酒南徐
聽夜雨江聲千尺。
記當年阿童東下
佛狸深入。
白面書生成底用
蕭郎裙屐偏輕敵。
笑風流北府好談兵
參軍客。

人事改　寒雲白。
舊壘廢　神鴉集。
儘沙沈浪洗
斷戈殘戟。
落日樓船鳴鐵鎖
西風吹盡王侯宅。
任黃蘆苦竹打寒潮
漁樵笛。

10　賀新郎　　病中有感

萬事催華髮。
論龔生, 天年竟天
高名難沒。
吾病難將醫藥治
耿耿胸中熱血。
待灑向, 西風殘月。
剖卻心肝今置地
問華佗解我腸千結。
追亡恨　倍淒咽。

故人慷慨多奇節。
為當年, 沈吟不斷
草間偷活。
艾灸眉頭瓜噴鼻
今日須難決絕。
早惠苦, 重來千疊。
脫屣妻孥非易事
竟一錢不值何須說。
人世事　幾完缺。

11　生查子　　旅思

一尺過江山
萬點長淮樹。
石上水潺潺
流入青谿去。

六月北風寒
落葉無朝暮。
度樾與穿雲
林黑行人顧。

12　臨江仙　　過嘉定,感懷侯研德

苦竹編籬茅覆瓦
海田久廢重耕。
相逢還說廿年兵。
寒潮衝戰骨
野火起空城。

門戶凋殘賓客在
淒涼侍酒侯生。
西風又起不勝情。
一篇思舊賦
故國與浮名。

13　蝶戀花　　　君山浮黛…

渺渺扁舟天一瞬。
極目空清
只覺雲根近。
片影參差浮復隱。
琉璃淨掛青螺印。

憶自嬴皇相借問。
堯女含顰
蘭珮悲荒燐。
淚竹千竿垂紫暈。
賓鴻不寄蒼梧信。

14　摸魚兒　　　東州桃浪

翦中流
白蘋芳草
燕尾江分南浦。
盈盈待學春花靨
人面年年如故。
留春住。
笑幾許浮萍
舊夢迷殘絮。
棠橈無數。
儘泛月蓮舒
留仙裙在
載取春歸去。

佳麗地
仙院迢遙煙霧。
溼香飛上丹戶。
蘸檀珠斗踈燈映
共作一天花雨。
君莫訴。
君不見
桃根已失江南渡。
風狂雨妒。
便萬點落英
幾灣流水
不是避秦路。

王夫之

15　青玉案　　　憶舊

桃花春水湘水渡。
縱一艇　迢迢去。
落日穎光搖遠浦。
風中飛絮
雲邊歸雁
盡指天涯路。

故人知我年華暮。
唱徹瀟陵回首句。
花落風狂春不住。
如今更老
佳期逾杳
誰倩啼鵑訴。

16　天仙子　　　元夕

垂垂凍雨凌珠滴。
阿誰喚作燈花夕。
當時有夢到今圓
孤烟冪。殘膏膩。
寒山不着東風力。

纜領取，歸鴻嘹嚦。
又消受，殘梅狼籍。
人間昨日是元宵
人非昔。天難識。
明年消盡中國歷。

17　卜算子　　詠傀儡, 示從遊諸子

也似帶春愁
卻倩何人説。
更無半字與關心
吐出丁香舌。

紅燭影搖風
斜映朦朧月。
鉛華誰辨假中真
皮下無點血。

18　女冠子　　賣薑詞

賣薑來也。
誰是能酬價者。
不須慳。
老去絲尤密
酸來心愈丹。

垂涎休自悶
有淚也須彈。
最療人間病
乍炎寒。

19　菩薩蠻　　述懷

萬心拋付孤心冷。
鏡花開落原無影。
只有一絲牽。
齊州萬點烟。

蒼烟飛不起。
花落隨流水。
石爛海還枯。
孤心一點孤。

陳維崧

20　賀新郎　　秋夜呈芝麓先生

擲帽悲歌發。
正倚幌, 孤秋獨眺
鳳城雙闕。
一片玉河橋下水
宛轉玲瓏如雪。
其上有秦時明月。
我在京華淪落久
恨吳鹽只點離人髮。
家何在　在天末。

馮高對景心俱折。
關情處, 燕昭樂毅
一時人物。
白雁橫天如箭叫
叫盡古今豪傑。
都只被, 江山磨滅。
明到無終山下去
拓弓弦, 渴飲黃羊血。
長楊賦　竟何益。

21　好事近　　夏日史蘧庵先生招飲…

分手柳花天
雪向晴窗飄落。
轉眼葵肌初綉
又紅敧闌角。

別來世事一番新
只吾徒猶昨。
話到英雄失路
忽涼風索索。

22　夏初臨　　本意。癸丑三月十九日，用明楊孟載韻

中酒心情
拆綿時節
蕡騰剛送春歸。
一畝池塘
綠陰濃觸簾衣。
柳花攪亂晴暉。
更畫梁，玉翦交飛。
販茶船重
挑筍人忙
山市成圍。

舊然卻想
三十年前
銅駝恨積
金谷人稀。
劃殘竹粉
舊愁寫向闌西。
惆悵移時
鎮無聊，搯損薔薇。
許誰知。
細柳新蒲
都付鵑啼。

23　卜算子　　阻風瓜步

風急楚天秋
日落吳山暮。
鳥柏紅梨樹樹霜
船在霜中住。

極目落帆亭
側聽催船鼓。
聞道長江日夜流
何不流儂去。

24　清平樂　　夜飲友人別館，聽年少彈三弦

簷前雨罷。
一陣淒涼話。
城上老烏啼啞啞。
街鼓已經三打。

漫勞醉墨紗籠。
且娛別院歌鐘。
怪底燭花怒裂
小樓吼起霜風。

25　江南春　　和倪雲林韻

風光三月連櫻筍
美人躊躇白日靜。
小屏空翠颭東風
不見其餘見衫影。
無端料峭春閨冷。
忽憶青驄別鄉井。
長將妾淚黦紅巾。
願作征夫東畔塵。

人歸遲　春去急。
雨絲滿院流光溼。
錦書道遠嗟莫及。
坐守吳山一春碧。
何日功成還馬邑。
雙倚枇杷花樹立。
夕陽飛絮化為萍。
攬之不得徒營營。

26　過澗歇　　顯德寺前看楓葉

嵐翠濃於草鞋夾。
繞坡細流
潚潚暗通苔雲。
谷聲遲。
下落亂泉聲裏
愀悄如相答。
此間景
純得關仝巨然法。

寺松三百本
雨溜蒼皮
霜彫黛甲。
禿榦爭敧壓。
笑語同遊
黃葉鳴簷
丹楓裹寺
如何不荷埋身錨。

朱彝尊

27　滿江紅　　吳大帝廟

玉座苔衣
拜遺像紫髯如昨。
想當日周郎陸弟
一時聲價。
乞食肯從張子布
舉杯但屬甘興霸。
看尋常談笑敵曹劉
分區夏。

南北限　長江跨。
樓櫓動　降旗詐。
歎六朝割據
後來誰亞。
原廟尚存龍虎地
春秋未輟雞豚社。
膡山圍衰草女牆空
寒潮打。

28　賣花聲　　雨花臺

衰柳白門灣。
潮打城還。
小長干接大長干。
歌板酒旗零落盡
膡有漁竿。

秋草六朝寒。
花雨空壇。
更無人處一憑闌。
燕子斜陽來又去
如此江山。

29　蝶戀花　　重游晉祠題壁

十里浮嵐山近遠。
小雨初收，最喜春沙軟。
又是芳草天涯遍。
年年汾水看歸雁。

繫馬青松猶在眼。
勝地重來，暗記韶華變。
依舊紛紛涼月滿。
照人獨上溪橋畔。

30　長亭怨慢　　雁

結多少，悲秋儔侶。
特地年年
北風吹度。
紫塞門孤
金河月冷
恨誰訴。
迴汀枉渚。
也只戀，江南住。
隨意落平沙
巧排作，參差箏柱。

別浦。
慣驚移莫定
應怯敗荷疏雨。
一繩雲杪
看字字，懸鍼垂露。
漸剺斜，無力低飄
正目送，碧羅天暮。
寫不了相思
又蘸涼波飛去。

31　春風裊娜　　游絲

倩東君著力
繫住韶華。
穿小徑　漾晴沙。
正陰雲籠日
難尋野馬
輕颺染草
細綰秋蛇。
燕蹴還低
鶯銜忽溜
惹卻黃鬚無數花。
縱許悠揚度朱戶
終愁人影隔窗紗。

惆悵謝娘池閣
湘簾乍捲
凝斜盼，近拂簷牙。
疏籬胃　短牆遮。
微風別院
好景誰家。
紅袖招時　偏隨羅扇
玉鞭墮處　又逐香車。
休憎輕薄
笑多情似我
春心不定
飛夢天涯。

32　卜算子

殘夢繞屏山
小篆消香霧。
鎮日簾櫳一片垂
燕語人無語。

庭草已含烟
門柳將飄絮。
聽徧梨花昨夜風
今夜黃昏雨。

33　搗練子

烟娟娟，雨綿綿。
花外東風冷杜鵑。

獨上小樓人不見
斷腸春色又今年。

34   水龍吟   謁張子房祠

當年博浪金椎　　　　遺廟彭城舊里。
惜乎不中秦皇帝。　　有蒼苔，斷碑橫地。
咸陽大索　　　　　　千盤驛路
下邳亡命　　　　　　滿山楓葉
全身非易。　　　　　一灣河水。
縱漢當興　　　　　　滄海人歸
使韓成在　　　　　　圯橋石杳
肯臣劉季。　　　　　古牆空閉。
算論功三傑　　　　　悵蕭蕭白髮
封留萬戶　　　　　　經過孳涕
都未是　平生意。　　向斜陽裏。

納蘭性德

35   南鄉子   為亡婦題照

淚咽卻無聲。　　　　別語忐分明。
只向從前悔薄情。　　午夜鶼鶼夢早醒。
憑伏丹青重省識　　　卿自早醒儂自夢
盈盈。　　　　　　　更更。
一片傷心畫不成。　　泣盡風簷夜雨鈴。

36   如夢令

萬悵穹廬人醉。　　　還睡。
星影搖搖欲墜。　　　還睡。
歸夢隔狼河　　　　　解道醒來無味。
又被河聲攪碎。

37   金縷曲   贈梁汾

德也狂生耳。　　　　共君此夜須沈醉。
偶然間，緇塵京國　　且由他，蛾眉謠詠
烏衣門弟。　　　　　古今同忌。
有酒惟澆趙州土　　　身世悠悠何足問
誰會成生此意。　　　冷笑置之而已。
不信道，遂成知己。　尋思起，從頭翻悔。
青眼高歌俱未老　　　一日心期千劫在
向尊前，拭盡英雄淚。後身緣，恐結他生裏。
君不見　月如水。　　然諾重，君須記。

38　臨江仙　　寒柳

飛絮飛花何處是　　　　　最是縈絲搖落後
層冰積雪摧殘。　　　　　轉教人憶春山。
疏疏一樹五更寒。　　　　湔裙夢斷續應難。
愛他明月好　　　　　　　西風多少恨
憔悴也相關。　　　　　　吹不散眉彎。

39　蝶戀花　　出塞

今古河山無定數。　　　　幽怨從前何處訴。
畫角聲中　　　　　　　　鐵馬金戈
牧馬頻來去。　　　　　　青塚黃昏路。
滿目荒涼誰可語。　　　　一往情深深幾許。
西風吹老丹楓樹。　　　　深山夕照深秋雨。

40　浣溪沙　　西郊馮園看海棠，因憶香嚴詞。有感

誰道飄零不可憐。　　　　一片暈紅才著雨。
舊游時節好花天。　　　　幾絲柔柳乍和烟。
斷腸人去自經年。　　　　倩魂銷盡夕陽前。

41　酒泉子

謝卻荼蘼。　　　　　　　嬾寒無賴羅衣薄。
一片明月如水。　　　　　休傍闌干角。
篆香消　猶未睡。　　　　最愁人　鐙欲落。
早鴉啼。　　　　　　　　雁還飛。

李雯

42　菩薩蠻　　懷未來人

薔薇未洗胭脂雨。　　　　斜陽芳草隔。
東風不合催人去。　　　　滿目傷心碧。
心事兩朦朧。　　　　　　不語問青山。
玉簫春夢中。　　　　　　青山響杜鵑。

王士禎

43　浣溪沙　　紅橋同籜庵，茶村，伯璣，其年，秋崖賦

北郭青溪一帶流。
紅橋風物眼中秋。
綠楊城郭是揚州。

西望雷塘何處是。
香魂零落使人愁。
澹烟芳草舊迷樓。

44　蝶戀花　　和漱玉詞

涼夜沈沈花漏凍。
欹枕無眠
漸聽荒雞動。
此際閒愁郎不共。
月移窗罅春寒重。

憶共錦衾無半縫。
郎似桐花
妾似桐花鳳。
往事迢迢徒入夢。
銀箏斷續連珠弄。

曹貞吉

45　留客住　　鵪鴣

瘴雲苦。
徧五溪，沙明水碧
聲聲不斷
只勸行人休去。
行人今古如織
正復何事關卿
頻寄語
空祠廢驛
便征衫溼盡
馬蹄難駐。

風更雨。
一髮中原　杳無望處。
萬里炎荒
遮莫摧殘毛羽。
記否越王春殿
宮女如花
祇今惟賸汝。
子規聲續
想江深月黑
低頭臣甫。

顧貞觀

46　夜行船　　鬱孤臺

為問鬱然孤峙者。
有誰來，雪天月夜。
五嶺南橫
七閩東距
終古江山如畫。

百感茫茫交集也。
憺忘歸，夕陽西掛
爾許雄心
無端客淚
一十八灘流下。

Index

David R. Mc Craw received his Ph.D. from Stanford University, where he studied with the late James J. Y. Liu. Currently assistant professor of Chinese at the University of Hawaii, he has published articles on several Chinese poets and is completing a book on Du Fu's regulated verse.

Production Notes

This book was designed by Roger Eggers.
Composition and paging were done on the
Quadex Composing System and typesetting
on the Compugraphic 8400 by the design
and production staff of University of
Hawaii Press.

The text typeface is Baskerville
and the display typeface is Schneidler.
Offset presswork and binding were done by
Vail-Ballou Press, Inc. Text paper is
Glatfelter Offset Vellum, basis 50.